"If I could give one book to Everyday Heroism by Christine Hanus would be it. As wise as it is humorous, this heart-to-heart meditation is guaranteed to cheer and inspire those who do the deepest work of all: mothers."
—**Mary Eberstadt**
Author of *Adam and Eve after the Pill, Revisited*

"Christine writes from the heart in *Everyday Heroism*. The illustrations of grace that come from the "little way" of being a mom fill each page. The scripture, words of the saints, and prayers for each day are enriching. Whether a new mom or a seasoned mother in need of refreshment, you will be blessed by these day-by-day meditations."
—**Very Rev. Malachi Van Tassell, T.O.R., Ph.D.**
President, Saint Francis University

"Funny, humble, warm, wise—Christine Hanus manages to be all these things to the mother in the trenches. In a world of Instagram feeds filled with false images of perfection, her words are refreshing and necessary, and will doubtless save many moms from despairing, "Am I the only one?" I am often asked by women where they can find a spiritual director—and while nothing can take the place of an actual person, this book is a great place to start for any mother seeking a guide. I can't recommend it enough."
—**Claire Dwyer**
Author of *This Present Paradise: A Spiritual Journey with St. Elizabeth of the Trinity* and editor of Spiritualdirection.com

Everyday Heroism

*28 Daily Reflections on the
Little Way of Motherhood*

Christine M. Hanus

Copyright ©2023 Christine M. Hanus
All Rights Reserved.

Scripture quotations contained herein are taken from the Revised Standard Version-Second Catholic Edition.

ISBN: 979-8-9881301-0-9

For more information, please visit **christinehanus.com**.

Printed in the United States of America

Contents

✷

A Note to the Reader 1

Part I: Laying a Foundation

Day One: *A Deep Breath* 7

Day Two: *A Different Kind of Hero* 11

Day Three: *Motherhood—from Heaven's Perspective* . . 15

Day Four: *Dreams that Matter* 21

Day Five: *The "Way"* 25

Day Six: *Overcoming Barriers—True Freedom* 31

Day Seven: *A Deliberate Decision* 35

Part II: Living It Out in the Everyday

Day Eight: *Humility and Who We Really Are* . . . 43

Day Nine: *Love, True Love* 49

Day Ten: *Praying Daily* 55

Day Eleven: *Praying Daily, Continued* 61

Day Twelve: *Praying as a Family* 65

Day Thirteen: *Praying the Mass* 69

Day Fourteen: *Works—Embracing Motherhood.* . . . 75

Day Fifteen: *Works—Evidence of Love* 79

Day Sixteen: *Works—A Cup of Confusion* 83

Day Seventeen: *Works—A Cup of Confusion, Continued* . 87

Day Eighteen: *Joy—The Natural Result of the "Little Way"*. . 91

Day Nineteen: *Joy—Be Grateful* 95

Day Twenty: *Joy—Choose It or Lose It* 101

Day Twenty-One: *Sorrows and Sufferings—
Little Things Add Up* 107

Day Twenty-Two: *Sorrows and Sufferings—
When it Really Hurts.* 113

Day Twenty-Three: *Sorrows and Sufferings—
On the Cross* 119

Day Twenty-Four: *Setting the World Ablaze* 123

Part III: Teenagers, Education, and Mission

Day Twenty-Five: *The Teen Years* 129

Day Twenty-Six: *Taking the Wheel* 135

Day Twenty-Seven: *Messy, Mysterious, and Entrusted
with a Mission* 141

Day Twenty-Eight: *More Than Diplomas and Tight Abs* . 147

About the Author 151

It is necessary that the heroic becomes daily and that the daily becomes heroic.

—St. Zelie Martin
(St. Thérèse of Liseaux's mother)

A Note to the Reader

✳

*D*ear Fellow Moms,

    There are two reasons I wrote this book. It all started with my own struggles as I began to live out the heroic call to motherhood, which was a lot less idyllic than I first imagined it would be. My head knew how significant my vocation was, but there was always a part of me that fought the obscurity and mundaneness of it all, especially when the kids were very young. I started journaling about my experiences to encourage myself and to remind myself why I was eager to be a mom in the first place.

    Second, as many of the women I knew started to marry, I became increasingly aware of the dilemma women face. I realized there were women who wanted to be good wives and mothers as much as I did, but their cultural education had omitted, warped, and even disparaged a Catholic understanding of what it means to be a woman. So I began writing to offer women something practical, beautiful, and eternal—a Catholic perspective on motherhood.

When I started to write this book about embracing motherhood while in the *midst* of it, something interesting happened: the time and energy necessary to write any kind of book was impossible for me to find. Like taking a long shower or having nice furniture ... it just wasn't happenin'. Paradoxically, the longer I went without realizing my dream of producing a book that examines what I call "the little way of motherhood," the more qualified I became! My youngest child is now eighteen. And no, I haven't brought home a paycheck or earned a degree in more than twenty years. I haven't accomplished many of my goals—or the thinness—I had planned for myself. Yet, being "unsuccessful" in the eyes of the world does add to my credibility when speaking about the Little Way. When I claim that a life lived in service to family is grossly undervalued in our culture, I can now personally testify to the fruit it bears over time.

Recently, though, I did find the time to finish this book. In fact, it was my oldest son, now twenty-seven years old, who kept urging me to finish it.

I have written from the heart, often sharing my own story as an ordinary Catholic mom. I have thought of you often over the past fifteen years—you women who are now reading this book—and I am praying God's best for you and your families. As you read, reflect, and pray over the course of the next twenty-eight days (or however you choose to break it up), I hope that God will help you internalize whatever is most helpful in these pages.

Finally, though this series of reflections is for *any* mother who wants to be encouraged and renewed in her vocation as a mom—or for any woman who wants to understand more about the true meaning and purpose of motherhood—it is written with special empathy and encouragement for the women who are in the midst of kid-chaos. Kid-chaos is like childbirth. You forget the intensity of it when you are no longer being overpowered by it. One day, in the not too distant future, you will look back at the present frenzied pandemonium of your family life and say, "Ahhh ... those were the days!" In the meantime, there is so much to be grateful for and so much good work you are doing.

To all moms everywhere, be assured, God has an amazing purpose and plan for your life.

Love on!

Christine

P.S. It was difficult for me to so often leave husbands out of the conversation in these meditations, but I wanted this book to be for single moms as well as married. In an effort to support and validate the heroic work of many single parents, sometimes the other parent (dads in particular) are treated as superfluous. They are a far cry from superfluous!

Let it be known in no uncertain terms: the sacrament of marriage is the primary well-spring of the grace we need to parent. God looks after single parents and their children in a particularly powerful way, but marriage was instituted by Christ as a sacrament for a reason! *The sacrament of Matrimony is the normative way for parents to receive the grace necessary to parent well.*

PART I

Laying a Foundation

Jesus said, "Every one then who hears these words of mine and does them will be like a wise man who built his house upon the rock; and the rain fell, and the floods came, and the winds blew and beat upon that house, but it did not fall, because it had been founded on the rock."
Matthew 7:24-25

Day One

A Deep Breath

Life today is too busy, too noisy, and too complicated. Sometimes it helps to slow down and take a deep breath.

I hope that this book—with its twenty-eight short reflections designed to inspire you, offer you some insight about motherhood, and make you smile—can help you take that deep breath. After you read the daily reflection, spend a few moments meditating on the quote and short prayer at the end of each entry. This is where, whether you are inexperienced in prayer or have been developing a prayer life for many years, God wants to meet you and speak to you. The idea is to give each "day" at least fifteen minutes of your undivided attention for twenty-eight days. God is worth it, and so are you.

I chose the words "everyday heroism" for the title of this series of reflections because dedicated mothers are indeed heroes, and we need to be reminded just how irreplaceable moms are. If you have watched the quirky animated film

Megamind, you see how ugly it gets when heroes find their tasks *too* burdensome, *too* mundane … and stop showing up. When mothers lose sight of the significance of what they do and no longer do it well, all hell breaks loose.

It is also my hope that this series of reflections will take you on an inspiring, encouraging journey of the mind and heart. Let's face it, mothers get worn out. We need refreshment, rest, and encouragement. But, unfortunately, our world is so full of false remedies and temporary fixes, we may think all we need is a pedicure, a mixed drink, and a visit with our therapist or chiropractor, and we will be back in business. As helpful as these remedies can be for Worn-Out Mom, often the most effective solution of all remains untapped. For what we really need is *time* to sit in the warm, healing presence of our loving God. He is the One who made us and the One who can fix us. We also need time to think clearly, reasonably, and truthfully about our lives and our priorities and challenge ourselves to be rid of the dross that keeps us from finding true happiness.

Motherhood is a unique experience for every woman. In the process of writing this book, there have been times when, discouraged by my own failings as a mom and as a Catholic woman, I've put my pen down in shame. But I always pick it up again (as soon as I can find it amidst the debris and rubble), compelled to offer an encouraging vision of motherhood, viewed in the light of Scripture and the teaching and wisdom of the Catholic Church. As I continue traveling the road of motherhood myself, I extend the hand of sisterhood to you. We are all in this together!

In the next few weeks, I will often refer to the example or words of the saints. They are our older brothers and sisters who are alive in heaven and rooting for us. Talk about companions on the journey! In particular, Mary, the mother of Jesus, is really and truly our devoted and loving spiritual mother (see Revelation 12:17). God gave her this maternal role. He uses her motherly love and care to soften our hearts when, in our broken humanity, we would foolishly avoid God. To fail to ask for her intercession is to reject one of the greatest gifts God provides to bring us quickly into a loving relationship with himself. In my personal experience, there is something about Mary that has made me deeply aware that I am but a little child, and I must trust my Father and his love for me.

Meditate

Therefore, since we are surrounded by so great a cloud of witnesses, let us also lay aside every weight, and sin which clings so closely, and let us run with perseverance the race that is set before us, looking to Jesus the pioneer and perfecter of our faith.

Hebrews 12:1-2

Consider

Though the saint knows the mountain of God's love from having lived on its heights, the pilgrim in the valley can at least see the mountain and appreciate its grandeur from a distance. He or she can call out to other pilgrims and tell them of life lived on the heights.

Peter Kreeft

Pray

Dear Heavenly Father, please help me take time to intentionally sit in your presence as I begin this 28-day reflection on my vocation as a mother. I believe that you can and will help me in my daily life.

· · · · ·

Day Two

A Different Kind of Hero

I remember that day well, though it was not unusual.

It was seven a.m., and the kitchen floor, no matter how often I mopped the spot where the juice spilled, remained inexplicably sticky. The laundry was piled so high that Gabriel, my pre-schooler, was climbing it and victoriously sticking a flag (a pair of briefs on a sword) into its peak. Meanwhile, the elusive mouse in the hall closet startled me periodically, sending me scrambling up on a chair, while my sons laughed derisively.

As we started our day, which at that time in my life began with getting the oldest three ready for school, my children were rousing the worst in me. Did they have too much sugar last night? Not enough sleep? Whatever was causing it, they were all dialed up a notch. Mindful of Mary Catherine, the sleeping baby, I hushed them in vehement whispers — the kind that injure your throat.

As they ate breakfast, Patrick, my oldest child at twelve years of age, was in a goofy mood. He repeatedly tipped on his chair and was finally instructed to stand while eating—a posture that only intensified his comedic routine. Captivated by this budding Jim Gaffigan, the other boys snorted orange juice out their noses with each new bout of hilarity.

Sean, my second-oldest, ignored my plea to eat quickly, and nibbled leisurely at his bagel. Dominic, nine years old, bragged loudly about the pre-packaged lunch he had recently received for his birthday and was bringing to school that day. The minutes rapidly disappeared, and we were now running late. My commands become more sharp, more shrill, more frenzied.

Finally, eyes ablaze, I viciously scraped an entire row of stars off the "good behavior" chart hanging on the refrigerator and sent the three oldest off to brush their teeth.

Moments later, someone shrieked from the upstairs bathroom—the one right next door to the sleeping baby's room. Kicking slippers off my feet, I bolted up the stairs to learn that Dominic had been "hoarding the toothpaste," but Patrick informed me he had things under control, having successfully pinned Dominic to the edge of the tub in a wrestling hold.

Downstairs again, I frantically tried to finish packing lunches, pleading with the older boys to help out. Sean opened the freezer to find the ice packs, saying, "I'll help, Mom, don't worry." But the next thing I knew, he was stuffing one of the icepacks under his armpit and buttoning up his school sweater over it.

With a final promise of extra chores for a variety of infractions, I crammed a winter hat onto Patrick's carefully groomed hair. Feeling distinctly hypocritical, I led them in a short prayer and shepherded them out the door into the uncertainties and dangers of the world. As they walked the short distance to school, I sat at the crumb-covered kitchen table and ate a cold, mutilated bagel, while wondering just what kind of mother and person I was becoming.

When we women embark on the journey of motherhood, when we dare to dream the dream of a beautiful family and deep personal fulfillment, this type of scenario is not at the forefront of our minds. Becoming mothers for the first time, many of us feel a profound sense of destiny and purpose, but as we move into the thick of being "mom," we can quickly wake up to the reality of the daily struggle. We may find ourselves feeling trapped, confused (where did I go wrong?), and weary. We may suspect that family life is just too messy to be meaningful and doubt whether motherhood is making us into the kind of person we want to be. Heroic? Hardly!

Ultimately, we want to be great moms with fantastic kids. We want to be confident and happy. We want to be drawing closer to God, developing a relationship with him that goes beyond the niceties of "Now I lay me down to sleep." But, as with any really good thing, reaching these goals takes effort and time. The good news is we have a loving God who wants us to succeed. He invites us to open our minds to what "everyday heroism" looks like and open our hearts to his wisdom. This process begins by taking a step back in order to gain a fresh perspective on motherhood.

Meditate

He who began a good work in you will bring it to completion at the day of Jesus Christ.

Philippians 1:6

Consider

Love our Lady. And she will obtain abundant grace to help you conquer in your daily struggle.

St. Josemaría Escrivá

Pray

Dear God, in the times of chaos, in the moments when family life seems to be a cosmic joke and all of my lofty ideas go out the window, help me in those very moments to realize that you are doing a mighty work in and through me and that "everyday heroes" come in all shapes and sizes.

Dear Blessed Mother, pray for me!

* * * * *

Day Three

Motherhood—from Heaven's Perspective

Gianna Molla (1922–1962) was an extraordinary woman whose love for God and devotion to prayer and the Eucharist enabled her to be a physician who served the poor and troubled with compassion. She married in her thirties and quickly had three young children, but with live-in help was able to continue her medical practice.

During her fourth pregnancy, Gianna faced a dilemma. A tumor grew in her uterus. Gianna chose to save the life of her baby rather than have an abortion or a hysterectomy. The tumor was removed, but after the baby was born, Gianna suffered from an abdominal infection and soon died. She offered her body as a "living sacrifice" (see Romans 12:1) in a most profound way, in the service of life and for the love of her child. In her holiness within family life and in her service to others, she provides us with an inspiring example of how to be a woman of God. The Catholic Church declared her a saint in 2004.

Stories like this remind us just how radical and life-giving a mother's love can be. But while all good mothers know that we ought to be heroic for the sake of our children, most of us do not suffer such dramatic trials. Sometimes it is hard to see how the quiet, hidden ways in which we serve our families can possibly be as worthy of praise as St. Gianna's ultimate sacrifice.

The beauty and significance of motherhood is far too easily diminished because it is in one sense—and in the eyes of the world—ordinary. It is similar to the way we take the earth under our feet for granted. Whenever I look at images of earth taken from *space* I am always reminded that something breathtakingly miraculous is happening. Occasionally, it is necessary to step back and look at motherhood this way.

It is strange and disturbing that the vocation of motherhood (and fatherhood, too) is so little revered in our time and culture. Many young people have never been taught that children thrive best when they live with both their mother and their father and that the well-being of a child is directly linked to the intimacy of the family unit. Sociological studies prove it, science confirms it, and common sense—which is no longer very common—has known it all along.

Within the Christian tradition, parents are clearly expected to assume absolute primacy in the raising of their children, modeling self-donation and virtue and assisting their children in whatever way they can to be all that God has created them to be. Men and women do this each in their own way and, together, can impact their children in a way that no one else has the power to do.

Mothers, in particular, are the heart of the home. Their gifts tend to be revealed in the areas of nurturing, intuition, sympathy, communication, and conflict resolution. Their feminine smell, the softness of their skin and breasts, and their loveliness and other womanly qualities comfort their children and reveal to them something about God's love and beauty. A woman's ability to create a home—a place to recuperate and refocus, where love, attention, food, sleep, clean clothes, and other necessities are readily available—is foundational to the welfare of society itself. And let's not forget the woman's irreplaceable role in bringing children into the world in the first place!

The power to raise our children well is in our hands, but the time in which we have to do it is terribly short. I wrote the following when my children were tiny:

> As time goes by, I realize more and more the nature of the task of raising children. How quickly my children are growing! Now they depend on us for all; soon they will be independent. I'll respect them and love them as adults, and yet I will miss my babies, and I want to make the most of this fleeting opportunity to deeply experience motherhood. We have a very limited time to lay the foundations on which our children's lives will be built, but what an incredibly tender and needy period of life it is for them. This is also the moment to ensure that our relationship with them will continue into the future.

Now that my children are mostly grown, I see just how true my instincts were when I wrote this. I will never regret pouring myself into their upbringing.

There is no doubt that living out our call to motherhood for love of God and in service to others can sometimes feel mundane and uninspired. It can prevent us from reaching career goals or the personal goals we treasured before becoming mothers, back when we thought we could "do it all," and do it well. But if we live out this vocation faithfully, it can shape us into the kind of women we long to be and impact our families and the world in a way that surpasses our wildest dreams.

Throughout history, God has raised up so many extraordinary women to witness to the beauty and sacrificial love of motherhood. And some of them are the ones our world considers "ordinary"—like you and me.

Meditate

She looks well to the ways of her household, and does not eat the bread of idleness. Her children rise up and call her blessed; her husband also, and he praises her.

Proverbs 31:27-28

Consider

A mother's arms are made of tenderness and children sleep soundly in them.

Victor Hugo

Pray

God Almighty, help me to see the beauty of my femininity and the specific gifts I have and to use those gifts to bless my family. Enable me to see with new eyes the value of what I am doing for my family and for the world.

· · · · ·

Day Four

Dreams that Matter

I recently attended a high school graduation ceremony at a public school. Naturally, it was devoid of any mention of God other than in the Pledge of Allegiance. God, the author of the universe, created these young people out of nothing and brought them into being. He has a perfect plan for each of them, but his very name is taboo during one of the most significant moments of their lives. Instead, the speakers at the ceremony waxed poetic about "following your dreams," a theme lavishly incorporated into children's movies, television shows, and social media. Why is this?

As human beings, we instinctively know that we need direction on life's journey. Reaching out to God for his guidance is built into who we are. But when we don't submit ourselves to him—or purposefully shut him out—all we can come up with is, "Follow your dreams!" I wanted to jump up on my chair at this graduation ceremony and shout, "Enough of the fluffy crap that doesn't mean anything! Some dreams change according to what you have eaten the night before—*are you following dreams that are worth pursuing?!*" My children were grateful I didn't do this. (But I think my husband would have loved it. And recorded it.)

We all need to decide carefully which types of goals and dreams are really worth pursuing before making them the guiding principle of our lives. Having dreams is a very good thing, but when we passionately follow dreams without taking into account where we come from, where we are going, and why our dreams matter, we can quickly find ourselves on the wrong path—a path that may look pretty good at first, but eventually leads to regret and possibly tragedy.

We can make little progress in our mission as Catholic mothers unless we first ask ourselves an elemental question: Do the dreams we pursue reflect a foundational understanding of *who we are?*

We need to remind ourselves and each other that *we come from God and that he intends for us to live with him forever in heaven.* He is where we come from; he is where we are going.

We must make all of our life's choices based on that truth and the very real fact that *we are precious daughters of God.* He has a plan for each of us, and it often looks quite different from the picture of success that the world shows to us. We were not created to stand on the stage of life with happy tears streaming down our faces as Simon Cowell, from *America's Got Talent*, hits the Golden Buzzer. No, our destiny is far more significant than making a name for ourselves. *God has a much greater purpose and plan for us.*

These truths give us the clarity to know that the ultimate goal of our lives is to live for God—to *fulfill* his purpose and plan and to become who he is calling us to be. Only when we do this can we hope to grow more loving, capable, and interesting ... to live with strength and dignity and to laugh without fear when we look toward the future (see Proverbs 31:25).

We want to become virtuous, attractive women, filled with purpose—we want to be heroic. We want to be heroic so that our families can thrive and that, as a family, we can navigate this scary, fascinating world and live forever together with our loving Father in heaven.

So we must strive to cooperate with the grace that God gives us to live out the calling that he has on our lives: to grow in holiness, to be "perfected in love" and to accomplish his will. *This* is true heroism. *This* is the dream worth following with all of our energy—the one dream that will give us our best chance at happiness in this life and the next.

In the next reflection, we will think about what route we need to take in order to make this dream a reality.

Meditate

For I know the plans I have for you, says the Lord, plans for welfare and not for evil, to give you a future and a hope.

Jeremiah 29:11

Consider

Go ahead! Courage! In the spiritual life he who does not go forward goes backward.

St. Padre Pio

Pray

Come Holy Spirit, assist me in recognizing who I am in Christ and in choosing a dream that is worth pursuing. Help me work toward that which will bring me holiness and authentic happiness.

* * * * *

Day Five

The "Way"

Assuming that the dream we have for our lives is to become what God has called us to be, we have to decide how best to reach this goal. In one sense, this route is different for each of us, unique to our own situation. In another more general sense, God has explicitly revealed to us the route everyone must take if we are to come into a relationship with him. We will consider what that route is and, in the next reflection, examine misconceptions that can act as road blocks along this path. It is important to lay this foundation before moving on to the practical, daily ways we can live out our call to motherhood.

When I was a young teenager, I came to a startling realization that God was real and that he loved me. Because I was so young when I came into this intimate relationship with God, I enjoyed an uncomplicated faith that I sometimes have trouble practicing as an adult. As a young person, I felt particularly tuned into God and followed him with childlike simplicity.

During this period in my life, I was babysitting one evening during a thunderstorm. The children were safely in bed, but the earsplitting cracks of thunder and the frequent dazzling flashes of lightning made me uneasy and restless. The rambling house was in a secluded spot, which made me feel exposed and vulnerable. Then the lights went out. Heart pounding, I scrabbled through a couple of drawers as the lightning flashed, looking for a candle and wincing at the sound of each peal of thunder. Finding a candle, I searched in vain for a match or a lighter.

Finally, I gave up and groped around for a chair. Sitting down, perfectly still in the inky blackness, I began to pray. After a little while, I became aware of an internal urge telling me to stand up. I obeyed. Then the inspiration told me to walk forward. Feeling slightly ridiculous, I followed what became a step-by-step procedure, and when I "heard" the command to turn left and go down the stairs into the old part of the house, I did it. I was then prompted to turn and face the door which led outside, where an old coat hung on a hook. I was prompted once more, "Reach into the pocket of that coat." I reached into the pocket and grasped an object, identifying what it was almost before I touched it. One large wooden match.

Needless to say, I was delighted—giddy with God's provision and care for me, but at the same time, not surprised. For I had the faith of a child. I was confident in God's love for me. It is this kind of childlike response to the call of God in our lives that each of us seeking his will should embrace.

One saint that can help us understand this simple, but profound response to God is St. Thérèse of Lisieux, who is noted for her childlike spirituality and her "little way." As a mother, I have tried to apply some of her wisdom to my life, and have found it remarkably useful. Transformative, actually.

St. Thérèse was a young Carmelite nun who lived in France in the late 1800s. As a child, St. Thérèse received a good education and aspired to do "great" things for God, such as travel abroad as a missionary, and imagined serving God to the point of martyrdom.

Thérèse sought after the same thing everyone wants—the deep, abiding peace and joy that comes from understanding the purpose of her life. She was blessed to realize at a young age that these desires would only be satisfied by living a holy life ... by becoming a saint.

This pursuit of holiness was the key to everything.

But in her yearning for holiness, she was obliged to put aside her own preconceived notions as to what it meant to do something momentous with her life. Instead of becoming overwhelmed and discouraged by her faults and failings, or by her lack of accomplishments, she began to live out the Little Way.

In her autobiography, *Story of a Soul,* she said, "For me to become great is impossible. I must bear with myself and my many imperfections; but I will seek out a means of getting to Heaven by a little way—very short and very straight, a little way."[1]

In order to do this, she abandoned herself to God with the simplicity of a child, determined to perform her daily duties, many of them basic household tasks, for the love of God.

---

[1] St. Thérèse of Lisieux, *Story of a Soul*, chapter IX, section 3.

Thérèse once wrote in a letter to her younger sister, "Pick up a pin from a motive of love, and you may thereby convert a soul. Jesus alone can make our deeds of such worth, so let us love Him with every fibre of our heart" (January 1895, letter to Leonie).

Thérèse approached her relationships with the same zealous self-forgetfulness. Within the convent where she lived, Thérèse would allow others to judge her harshly and refuse to defend herself. If a fellow Carmelite sister in the convent annoyed her, Thérèse would bear it cheerfully. On one occasion, when she felt an antipathy toward another Carmelite sister, she went out of her way to serve her and to pray for her. Eventually, this sister said to Thérèse, "My dear Soeur Thérèse, tell me what attraction you find in me, for whenever we meet, you greet me with such a sweet smile." Thérèse tried to do everything with love.

Thérèse died at age twenty-four and never did anything that would mark her as "successful" in the eyes of the world. Nevertheless, she is looked upon by the Catholic Church in her littleness as an expert on the spiritual life, and when she said, "I want to spend my heaven in doing good on earth" she meant business. Countless miracles have been attributed to her intercession.

St. Thérèse's "way" brings fresh insight into what it means to strive for holiness and helps us more fully embrace humility and trust in God. This spirituality is particularly applicable to mothers who find themselves making many sacrifices, most of which go unrewarded in conventional ways. Yearning for greatness, most of us have a propensity to by-pass a simple way of living, thinking that somehow we have to *do more*, and *be more*, when all we really need to do is God's will.

This idea may initially seem straightforward and simple enough, but when the time comes to live the Little Way, we resist, because it involves dying to ourselves and relinquishing many of our own superficial desires. This is why many do not value the Little Way. The "easy way" and "my way" are much more popular mottoes.

One of my sons, at the age of four, would have worn his red Power Ranger T-shirt every day if we had let him. One time, he fished it out of the hamper and his dad caught him putting it on.

My husband, Pat, said, "Son, you cannot wear that shirt. It is dirty."

Defiantly, the small boy thrust the shirt into his dad's hands and demanded, "Show me."

Pat obliged him, and after a long, thinking pause, Gabriel snatched the shirt out of his dad's hands and took off running, shouting over his shoulder, "It's not *all* dirty!"

We adults, too, become attached to our lives the way they are, or even to our sin. We want to think of ourselves as heroic, but we don't want to change. We look at the people around us and think, "Comparatively, I am a really good person." We do not want to do things God's way.

The Little Way, which is so helpful for us to contemplate as mothers, is a participation in the reality of Jesus Christ, who is the Way, the Truth, and the Life (see John 14:6). Jesus trusted his Father completely and, by following him, we can develop the same trust that St. Thérèse developed. The Little

Way is an acknowledgment that, if we want to be holy, we must do God's will the best we can and trust our loving Father to aid us in our weakness.

Meditate

"Truly, I say to you, unless you turn and become like children, you will never enter the kingdom of heaven."

Matthew 18:3

Consider

Holiness is not a matter of any one particular method of spirituality: it is a disposition of the heart that makes us small and humble within the arms of God, aware of our weaknesses, but almost rashly confident in His Fatherly goodness.

St. Thérèse of Lisieux

Pray

Jesus, thank you for providing a clear path for me to follow. May I, like St. Thérèse, imitate your humility and self-sacrificial love. Give me the desire for holiness, so that I can find authentic happiness and fulfillment in this life and be with you forever in heaven.

Day Six

Overcoming Barriers—True Freedom

As we continue along the road to holiness in pursuit of our dreams, it is imperative that we ask ourselves if there may be road blocks along our route. What might be preventing us from fully surrendering to God with the trust of a child? And how might our ideas of autonomy and freedom contribute to the problem?

Many people refrain from surrendering themselves to God in a wholehearted way because they fear losing the ability to judge for themselves what will make them happy. This pseudo-freedom that both men and women buy into requires little self-denial or virtue. We simply identify ourselves as "a good person" by our own standards and act without regard to God's laws. Freedom has come to mean, "I can do what *I* think is best." Some may add the caveat, "as long as I'm not hurting anyone." While driving to meet up with my husband for lunch one day, I read this exact ideology on a bumper sticker. I lost my appetite.

Everyone is hurt when we make ourselves the arbiters of what is right and wrong. If we really want to become who we are called to be and experience God's blessing on our lives, we have to start by asking ourselves if *we* have this distorted idea of freedom.

In stark contrast to this definition of freedom, *the Christian definition of freedom is the ability to choose the good.* To choose what will ultimately lead to a positive end result, which often involves self-discipline and sacrifice in the short term.

We all deal in varying degrees with an inability to "choose the good" because of unhealthy habits or attachments, which are often sinful. So, ironically, and perfectly in accord with Satan's diabolical plan for us, the more we embrace the world's idea of freedom, by deciding for ourselves what is right and wrong, the more we sin. The more we sin, the less free we really are!

Whether it is an addiction to drugs, pornography, or food, most people will acknowledge that an addict is certainly not free, but the same can be said for the person who is controlled by the desire for material goods, the need for recognition, or the lure of entertainment. We all stand in need of a Savior who can free us from unhealthy thoughts, behavior, and attachments. God understands we are fallen human beings, and he wants to bring us into a relationship with himself, so that we can experience true freedom and begin to thrive.

I was giving my young son swimming lessons one day and, as he looked at his older brothers swimming and splashing and having a fine time, he kept begging, "Can I please have free time now? You said I could have free time if I practiced for a while." Finally, I gave in and allowed him his precious free time. He spent the next fifteen minutes hanging on to the pool ladder with an unhappy expression on his face, until he finally cried out in a cranky voice, "This is free? Just sitting here?"

I think this analogy is helpful in reference to the spiritual life. We want true freedom and, as Catholic women, we want our lives to really count for something in a world that seems to be settling for mediocrity with an imitation cherry on top. But we have no hope of reaching this goal if we sit back and refuse to act in obedience to God.

Beyond resisting our unhealthy attachments, continuing freedom requires additional, ongoing effort: active pursuit of what is good! Please keep this in mind as we move into the second part of this book (the day after tomorrow) because it is this effort that elevates our relationship with Christ, allowing us to pursue true freedom.

Meditate

For freedom Christ has set us free; stand fast therefore, and do not submit again to a yoke of slavery.

Galatians 5:1

Consider

In the royal galley of Divine Love, there are no galley slaves: all the rowers are volunteers.

St. Francis de Sales

Pray

Dear Father, in this day and age in which freedom is misunderstood and abused, help me to want to understand and live by your definition of freedom and to trust that you always have my best interest in mind.

Day Seven

A Deliberate Decision

As we complete part one in this series of reflections on what it means to be an "everyday hero," let's pause to consider several key questions, so that we don't miss the obvious. Strangely enough, they are questions that the majority of Catholics, even those who sincerely practice their faith, never ask themselves point-blank:

Have I made a deliberate decision to surrender my life to God?

Do I believe a personal relationship with God is possible?

Have I consciously decided to be a disciple of Christ?

Have I embraced whole-heartedly my baptismal promises?

Or instead, do I withhold myself from a deeply personal relationship with God, because I do not fully trust him?

If you are withholding yourself from God, you are engaging in the original sin of Adam and Eve. In effect, God said to Adam and Eve, "Do you trust me? Do you trust that I know what is best for you and I will never lead you astray?" And they decided that they *did indeed* know better than God, and they disobeyed him. Huge mistake.

God yearns for us to respond to the invitation of his son Jesus, who became man to deliver us from the effects of that original sin and restore us to a loving, trusting relationship with the Father.

Over and over in Scripture and in the lives of the saints, we see a common theme, and it is so beautiful because it is so truthful: Life on this earth is fraught with troubles, but we can know the One who brings light out of darkness, and we can walk with him always and allow him to lead us, not only to peace and joy in this earthly life, but to eternal life in heaven.

Perhaps you have been consciously living for Christ for many years, perhaps not. Either way, the prayer following today's reflection is just one way to concretize our willingness to surrender to God. This kind of prayer helps us to fall more and more in love with God every day, as we witness the awesome effects of *real* freedom, as women and as mothers.

As I mentioned in the previous reflection, the decision to follow Christ is just the beginning of our pilgrimage of faith. We will continue to stumble and fall along the way, but forgiveness is always ours for the asking. Especially powerful is the gift of the sacrament of reconciliation! If you haven't been to confession in a while—don't walk—run to the nearest Catholic Church, receive this sacrament, and be healed! The evil one hates it when we make use of this amazing gift because it so effectively breaks his hold on us and drenches us with live-giving grace. (If you need help with confession, search "A Guide to Confession" online for a handy downloadable resource from the Knights of Columbus.)

Scripture leaves no room for doubt: Not only can we lose a saving relationship with Christ (see Romans 11:22, Galatians 5:4, 1 Corinthians 9:27), but we are expected to bear fruit as his disciples and to walk in increasing freedom. We are expected to strive for holiness, which is nothing more than making a consistent, daily effort to do God's will with love. In the days ahead, we will dive into the way motherhood is perfectly suited to help us do exactly that!

Meditate

And [Jesus] said to them, "Follow me, and I will make you fishers of men." Immediately they left their nets and followed him.

Matthew 4:19-20

Consider

The Lord never tires of forgiving, never! It is we who tire of asking his forgiveness.

Pope Francis

Pray

Loving Father,
I surrender to you today with all my heart and soul.
Please come into my heart in a deeper way. I say,
"Yes" to you today. I open all the secret places of my
heart to you and say, "Come on in." Jesus, you are
the Lord of my whole life. I believe in you and receive
you as my Lord and Savior. I hold nothing back.
Holy Spirit, bring me to a deeper conversion to the
person of Jesus Christ. I surrender all to you: my time,
my treasures, my talents, my health, my family, my
resources, my work, relationships, time management,
successes and failures. I release it and let it go.

I surrender my understanding of how things 'ought' to be, my choices and my will. I surrender to you the promises I have kept and the promises I have failed to keep. I surrender my weaknesses and strengths to you. I surrender my emotions, my fears, my insecurities, my sexuality. I especially surrender _____(Here mention other areas of surrender as the Holy Spirit reveals them to you.) Lord, I surrender my whole life to you, the past, the present, and the future. In sickness and in health, in life and in death, I belong to you. (Prayer found on spiritualdirection.com)

※ ※ ※ ※ ※

PART II

※

Living It Out in the Everyday

*As therefore you received Christ Jesus the Lord, so live in him,
rooted and built up in him and established in the faith.*
Colossians 2:6-7

Day Eight

Humility and Who We Really Are

Now let's get back to talking about just how marvelously the vocation of motherhood goes hand in hand with the Little Way (aka everyday heroism) and how this vocation can help us become who God made us to be.

When I had little children to care for all day long, every day, I experienced many moments of desperation in my role as a mother. My sister is a lot like me, poor thing. One day, as she was hammering a nail in the wall to hang a picture, one of her preschool-aged twins came rushing into the room saying, "Are you banging your head against the wall again, Mom?"

Sometimes a mother feels absolutely helpless as she tries to make sense of family life. The home seems to be a place where everyone she loves most gathers in perfect cooperation to annihilate all that she has struggled to create. Mom just keeps thinking, "Is this it? Months of pregnancy and potty-training, giving up my own interests and pouring out my love, and *this* is my family?"

Humility, seeing ourselves as we really are, is the first step in learning to live out motherhood heroically. Motherhood gives us opportunities galore to realize that we need to turn to God for the help we need.

I recorded this conversation with my eleven-year-old one day:

Mom (raising voice to be heard): Patrick, weren't you supposed to put this towel away? It is lying at the top of the stairs.

Patrick (from his room): What?! You told me to put it in the hamper if it was dirty and it is!

Mom: Is this the hamper?

Patrick: What?! I have to go all the way downstairs just to put a towel in the hamper?

Mom (tone becoming dangerous): Leaving it here where someone can trip over it and plunge to their death isn't the answer, is it? ... And watch your tone!

Patrick: What?! I had to pick up my Legos first, which were all over the place because *someone* was playing with them, which they are not supposed to be doing!

Mom (teeth now clenched): I said watch-the-way-you-are-talking-to-me! And stop saying, "What" before every comment or I am going to go maaaad!

This conversation should have never taken place.

I tell myself, "You are the parent! Don't enter into these kinds of fruitless dialogues. Take charge. Calmly make a request and allot consequences." It is as simple as that, right?

Before I had children I thought I was kind. I thought I was patient. I thought I worked well with others. I thought my education and life experience had equipped me to take this parenthood thing and run with it. Run like an Olympian with a lighted torch. Little did I know the kids would wield the torch, and I would spend all day running around after them and putting out fires.

We recognize this need for God's help anew when our children begin interacting more with the outside world. I have felt increasingly powerless as our family leaves the sanctuary of the home, and I have to constantly ask the Holy Spirit to give me courage and wisdom.

Frequently, I have to speak up in difficult or embarrassing situations. Teachers see me and say, "Oh, here comes that over-protective parent. Does she want her children to live in a bubble all of their lives?" No, I don't, but up through the third grade might be nice. Or my heart starts to beat hard and my hands get sweaty as I confront the store manager once again about the near-pornographic images and words at eye level to my young boys at the checkout stand. "Let's see," their little minds could be deliberating, "What do I want? A Twix bar, a lollipop, or a magazine that tells me 10 Dirty Ways to Have Sex?"

In these circumstances, we may ask ourselves, "Why would God want me to be constantly in over my head? Doesn't he want me to be happy and my children to be safe?" Although sometimes feelings of humiliation and powerlessness can indicate the need for us to make a change in our lives (become better disciplinarians, use our time more effectively, etc.), they always indicate our need for God. And it is through moments and circumstances like these that motherhood helps us see *who we really are.*

Floundering in our efforts to do what we know is the most significant work of our lives teaches us, as nothing else can, how weak and vulnerable we are. The "little way of motherhood" originates in humility, which is nothing more than a profound understanding that as smart, faithful, and organized as a mother may be, God is God, and she is but dust and ashes. This is balanced by the realization that she, herself, is a beloved child of God, and with his help can be "Mother" to her children like no one else can. Amidst the busyness and messiness of family life, she can be—as Scripture promises—transformed from "one degree of glory to another" (see 2 Corinthians 3:18).

Meditate

[The Lord] said to me, "My grace is sufficient for you, for my power is made perfect in weakness."

2 Corinthians 12:9

Consider

What was the life of Christ but a perpetual humiliation?

St. Vincent de Paul

Pray

Dear Lord, thank you for the gift of motherhood which daily reminds me how much I need a Savior. Help me turn to you every day in the knowledge of how very weak I am.

· · · · ·

Day Nine

Love, True Love

When we come to understand this acute need of a Savior in our lives, day-in-and-day-out, we will go looking for him in a way that we never have before. When we truly and wholeheartedly look for him, we will find him, love him, and *desire* to serve him.

If humility is the first step on the journey of the "little way of motherhood," love is its second distinguishing characteristic. It is the fuel that keeps us burning. Everything else we will ever need flows from this intimate, fruitful relationship with Divine Love. As we journey with our Lord through life, he will "perfect us in love."

When we become mothers, *it is critical that we come to a better understanding of what it means to love and serve God,* not only to fulfill God's plan for our own lives, but to fulfill our responsibility to our children—to teach them who God is and how to make sense of their lives.

There are many ways that our love of God can be immature. One way is illustrated by a conversation I overheard between my two oldest sons when they were six and seven years old. They were outside playing in our grassless yard in New Mexico. Sean, straddling the large outdoor garbage can that doubled as their yard toy, said off-handedly, "I don't love God."

Patrick, digging in the dirt, paused to admonish him, "You have to love God. If you don't, you will go to hell, which is a very bad place."

Sean immediately replied, "I love God."

We can say that we love God, but what we really mean is that we have a fear of punishment.

A second, and all too common way for us to say we "love" God, is analogous to Gabriel's shenanigans when he was four years old and was supposed to be in bed. One night he had come downstairs twice already, once for a drink and once for something he needed desperately (a matchbox car, perhaps? a toy head of C3P0?). Finally, on the third trip downstairs, perceiving that I was not happy with his behavior, he threw his chubby arms around me, squeezed me, and said, "Love is more importanter than going to bed, huh Mom?"

Gabriel mistakenly thought his hug, which he knows to be of great value to me, would make up for the fact that he was not being obedient. This is often how we treat God. We say we love him, but we do not obey him. This is not genuine love. In the Bible, Jesus tells us that if we love him, we will keep his commandments (see John 14:15).

Motherhood calls us to a mature understanding of love, which is deeply satisfying. It isn't a relationship based on fear, nor is it a sentimental presumption that we can never earn God's disapproval, because, after all, he is loving and forgiving.

The reality is: God has initiated a love relationship with us. He gives us the opportunity to have an intimate union with him. He gives us his "spiritual DNA" when we are reborn by baptism. Not only do we have the Holy Spirit living in us, but we have the sacraments, given to us by Jesus himself to pour out more of his life upon us—including his very own body and blood in the Eucharist! All that is left for us to do is respond.

The Catholic Church has a beautiful summary of the effects of this response by regular people like you and me (who are called the "laity") in the *Catechism of the Catholic Church*:

> Hence the laity, dedicated as they are to Christ and anointed by the Holy Spirit, are marvelously called and prepared so that even richer fruits of the Spirit may be produced in them. **For all their works, prayers, and apostolic undertakings, family and married life, daily work, relaxation of mind and body, if they are accomplished in the Spirit—indeed even the hardships of life if patiently born—all of these become spiritual sacrifices acceptable to God through Jesus Christ.** In the celebration of the Eucharist these may most fittingly be offered to the Father along with the body of the Lord. And so, worshiping everywhere by their holy actions, the

laity consecrate the world itself to God, everywhere offering worship by the holiness of their lives (CCC 901, emphasis added).

Responding to God's overture of love and to the grace he gives us to live holy lives has the power to make us "everyday heroes." In the following days, we will reflect on a prayer called the "Morning Offering," which will help us make this daily response in a concrete way. In the "Morning Offering", we find a summary of what we have as human beings to give to God—namely, our prayers, works, joys, sorrows, and sufferings.

We will consider each of these categories separately, even though they are often commingled, and we will think about how God can use our seemingly trivial daily offerings to transform us and to change the world!

Meditate

For God so loved the world that he gave his only begotten son, that whoever believes in him should not perish but have eternal life.

John 3:16

Consider

He loves us, he makes us see and experience His love, and since he has "loved us first," love can also blossom as a response in us.
Pope Emeritus Benedict XVI

Pray

Morning Offering

O Jesus, in union with your most precious blood
Poured out on the cross and offered in every Mass.
I offer you today my prayers, works,
joys, sorrows and sufferings.

For the praise of your holy name
And all the desires of your sacred heart.
For reparation of sins,
The conversion of sinners,
The union of all Christians,
And our final union with you in heaven.
Amen.

Day Ten

. . . . .

Praying Daily

The *Catechism of the Catholic Church* tells us about the vital connection between prayer and a relationship with God: "Prayer is the living relationship of the children of God with their Father who is good beyond measure, with his Son Jesus Christ and with the Holy Spirit" (CCC 2565). In essence, prayer is what makes possible our ability to embrace our beliefs and gives us the power to live them out.

Prayer is the linchpin for what we strive to give to God in the "Morning Offering," because everything—our works, joys, sorrows and suffering—can become prayer.

Ideally, prayer is a way of life, but committing to periods of prayer helps us build this all-the-time relationship. I especially had difficulty establishing a set prayer time as a young mom. There were times when I would awake determined to start my morning with a prayer time, but I could rarely make myself get out of bed before my children did. Two minutes into my meditations, Sean would sound the "baby-is-in-trouble" alert, and I would stumble into the kitchen to find breakfast cereal strewn all over the floor. Or I would try again a couple of hours later and have my new resolution interrupted by the telephone or baby with sore gums or a toddler proclaiming, "I hungry bad!" By the time I met all these needs, it was noon and "Dear Lord!" uttered with anything but pious reverence was the closest that I came to prayer.

Yet, there are scores of opportunities throughout the day to pray in small, but significant, ways. As we weave different kinds of prayer into our day, aided by God's grace, we will find ourselves weaving our entire day into our prayer. We must remember that prayer, above all, is a response to God's love, and we should not treat it like a burdensome duty.

In the hope that it will be valuable to the busy mom, I will share ten practical ways to pray (in no particular order), five today and five tomorrow. Pick just one new idea from the list and give it a try.

1. **Keep it short and sweet.** Say the name of Jesus frequently or come up with a simple prayer that is easily repeated, such as *Come, Holy Spirit* or the Jesus Prayer: *Lord Jesus Christ, Son of God, have mercy on me, a sinner.* I like to pray for each family member by saying their name and then the name of Jesus. I often do this while I am brushing my teeth!

2. **Use pictures and statues to prompt prayer.** My mother has a statue of the Blessed Mother on the shelf above her sink, and it always reminds me to say a Hail

Mary as I do the dishes. I have holy cards stuck in the cabinet doors above my sink, and they often inspire me to ask for the help of one of these saints.

3. **Pray the Liturgy of the Hours.** The Liturgy of the Hours is a compilation of daily prayer and readings, available in book form or as an app, which is particularly focused on the psalms. All Catholics are encouraged to make use of this beautiful form of prayer, though for priests and certain other religious it is mandatory. I wouldn't necessarily recommend this form of prayer for beginners, but would highly recommend to anyone a monthly publication called *Magnificat*, which incorporates some of the prayers in the Liturgy of the Hours and offers some beautiful reflections. It is a practical, inspiring guide to prayer.

4. **Write to God in a prayer journal.** This helps us to recognize not only our needs, but our deficiencies in how we actually communicate with God. For instance, we may notice ourselves constantly petitioning God as though he were a giant gumball machine in the sky, rarely thanking him or just telling him how much we love him. If you have a record of what you have prayed for in the past, journaling can also help you see how God has answered your prayer. We so often miss the big picture! This practice has bolstered my faith and helped me recognize what God is saying to me and how he has intervened in my life. Satan wants us to forget how faithful God is.

5. **Memorize Scripture and use it prayerfully.** Internalizing God's word through *praying* is life-changing. Feeling fragile? Philippians 4:13, which says, "I can do all things in [Christ] who strengthens me" can be today's response to those feelings. Isaiah 54:11 tells us that God's word accomplishes what he sends it forth to do, and, according to Hebrews 4:12, we can use his word, which is "living and active, sharper than any two-edged sword" to fight the battles of this life, especially the spiritual ones which are more common than most people realize.

Meditate

Rejoice always, pray constantly, give thanks in all circumstances; for this is the will of God in Christ Jesus for you.
1 Thessalonians 5:16-18

Consider

For me, prayer means launching out of the heart toward God; a cry of grateful love from the crest of joy or the trough of despair: it is a vast, supernatural force that opens out my heart and binds me close to Jesus.
St Thérèse of Lisieux

Pray

Dear God, convict me. Help me understand more completely how vital it is to commune with you on a daily basis.

Day Eleven

Praying Daily, Continued

Five more practical ways to pray:

1. ***Lectio Divina*** This is a term the Church uses to describe a method of prayer and meditation whereby we sit down in a quiet place, open our hearts to the Holy Spirit and read Scripture in a slow and methodical way, using our imagination and other faculties, to sink into the story or draw insights from the words of the inspired writers. *God speaks to us through prayer and Scripture. Lectio divina is a great way to tune in to him.*
2. **Pray the Rosary.** In some ways, praying the Rosary is similar to *lectio divina*, as it calls us to meditate on Scripture and the life of Christ and his mother, Mary, who is our mother and model for holiness. It is also versatile and becomes a perfect prayer for the busy mom who wants to pray and do a routine task at the same time. The rhythm of the rosary is a great way

for mothers to let go of their cares as they fall asleep at night.
3. **Visit the Lord in the Blessed Sacrament.** The Eucharist has transformative power that is nothing short of miraculous. Find a church which offers times of Eucharistic Adoration, with exposition of the sacred host in a monstrance, or simply visit the Eucharistic Jesus in the tabernacle. He is waiting for us there in every Catholic Church, all over the world.
4. **Pray in small groups.** Doing this is especially fruitful when praying for specific help (a physical or mental healing, help in times of crisis, etc.), and it has been an incredibly edifying experience for me personally. Praying with others allows the Holy Spirit to move in powerful ways, sometimes through the charismatic gifts, which we ignore to our detriment.
5. **Give God thanks.** Try to thank God for everything, especially when things go wrong! Corrie Ten Boom, in her book *The Hiding Place,* recounts how she and her sister suffered as prisoners in a Nazi concentration camp. Once, when they were moved into particularly overcrowded, filthy barracks, they tried to put into practice what they had read that morning in their Bible: "Give thanks to God in all circumstances." They even thanked him for the infestation of fleas! Later they learned that this infestation was the very reason their barracks were free from interference of the guards.

As a busy mom of young kids, I have been counseled that, as long as I pray throughout the day, I should not worry about setting aside a specific time to pray. And certainly, frequent conversation with God amidst our duties of the day is an essential part of everyday heroism. But following the example of Christ in Scripture and the example of the saints, we also need some quiet, one-on-one time with the Lord in order to refocus befuddled thoughts and create a vibrant relationship with the Father, with Jesus, and with the Holy Spirit.

On the other end of the spectrum, some mothers may struggle with feeling that prayer is higher in value than the ordinary duties of their lives—and become frustrated that they cannot devote more time to it. St. Frances of Rome, a dedicated wife and mother who desired to join a convent before she married, was once interrupted by her husband five times while reading the office of Our Lady. When she returned to her devotion, the print had turned to gold. She is quoted as saying, "Sometimes [a homemaker] must leave God at the altar to find Him in her housekeeping."

Meditate

And in the morning, a great while before day, [Jesus] rose and went out to a lonely place, and there he prayed.

Mark 1:35

Consider

Contemplation is nothing else but a secret, peaceful and loving infusion of God, which, if admitted, will set the soul on fire with the Spirit of love.

St. John of the Cross

Pray

Dear God, I want prayer to become something I yearn for; a way to recharge my batteries and receive all the advantages that come with being in an intimate relationship with you. Holy Spirit, give me the grace at key moments to choose to pray; teach me how to pray.

Day Twelve

Praying as a Family

Recently, I was sitting in a hospital waiting room being subjected to the incessant noise on the television, which kept playing the same programming every fifteen minutes (as if waiting for a loved one to undergo chemotherapy weren't disturbing enough). Repeatedly, a cheerful voice claimed, "The very best thing you can do for your children is to teach them to exercise and eat healthy." Every time I heard it, the statement bothered me, and I wanted to tell everyone in the waiting room, "That's actually not true. It is very good, but it is not the *best* thing we can do for our children. We are all going to die someday, and a healthy liver and glossy hair won't get you to heaven! We have to teach our children to have a relationship with God!"

As we find ways to be more prayerful ourselves, we should include our children in our efforts. One way we do this is to let them see how we turn to God for real solutions to real problems. They notice *everything*—and they will notice when we pray.

I have put a kneeler in my living room as a visual reminder of how to cope with my troubles. For example, when I lose something (such as my keys, my temper, or my mind), I might go there to pray. One time when the kneeler was in front of the picture window, I knelt down there and closed my eyes. When I opened them, I was a little startled to see my ten-year-old son standing directly in front of me on the other side of the window. He had given me a hard time that morning and now mouthed mournfully, "Did *I* make you pray?"

Whatever the reason, he noticed where I go to get my strength!

In addition to our own example, we can have special times of the day set aside for prayer as a family. Using these times to pray in diverse ways—morning prayer, noontime Angelus prayer, three o'clock "Divine Mercy" prayer, etc.—will lead our children to pray more consistently. And just sitting in silence and inviting the Holy Spirit to come be with us is a beautiful, non-verbal way to pray.

My absolute favorite way to pray as a family with young children is singing in the car. When my kids were little, we did this for hours on end during frequent road trips. Thankfully, there are many resources available to help parents sing with their children—everything from Christian radio to simple scriptural memorization songs to Gregorian chant. (If you want your children to participate, all of their electronic devices should be left at home or go in the trunk!)

Granted, at certain times in their young lives, we may find our children standing on their heads while mom or dad is reading to them out of the Bible, nodding off during the Mass, or bickering over who leads the next decade of the Rosary, but it is my experience that teaching our children to commune with God is not in vain, no matter how unorganized it might be. The fact is, they get addicted to prayer and cannot easily dismiss it from their lives. One night, after the children were in bed, I heard the sweet, soft tones of the hymn "More Precious Than Silver" drifting down the stairs. I tiptoed nearer and realized it was the angelic soprano voice of my rowdy, sports-minded, seven-year-old son, Dominic. I didn't even know he could sing like that!

Essentially, it is our God-given duty as parents to teach our children how to pray, and we neglect that instruction at the risk of their souls. I find that my children have always been quite willing to join in some small way with most of my and my husband's efforts to lead them in various types of prayer. It helps to get them started at a young age, talk to them about what prayer is, and employ different methods of prayer to engage them and inspire them to reach out to God themselves.

Meditate

Be filled with the Spirit, addressing one another in psalms and hymns and spiritual songs, singing and making melody to the Lord with all your heart.

Ephesians 5:18-19

Consider

When a child is given to his parents, a crown is made for that child in Heaven, and woe to the parents who raise a child without consciousness of that eternal crown!

Archbishop Fulton J. Sheen

Pray

Lord, God, I give you praise and I am humbled that you would entrust my children to me (and my husband). Help me to teach them to pray and to discern what kind of prayer may resonate most deeply with my children.

Day Thirteen

Praying the Mass

As Catholics, we know that the Mass is the highest form of prayer. Though it can be a chaotic time with children in tow, attending Mass is well worth any sacrifice we might have to make.

One Sunday, our family took a drive to Emmitsburg, Maryland, where an inspiring replica of the Lourdes Grotto has been built. Mass began, and the densely packed church was full of prayerful-looking families—no one chewing gum, wearing short shorts, or texting. There was a subliminal, my-family-is-holier-than-your-family feeling in the air (okay, it was probably just in my head), and I wanted my children to be particularly well-behaved.

As Mass began, it was clear Mary Catherine, who was two, was not on the same page as me. Typically, she followed along with the singing quite credibly, but on that particular day she was using her full lung capacity until her singing was more like sustained shouting.

As for the four boys, they couldn't sit still. Silently elbowing one another, they jockeyed for a position next to me, stepping on my sandaled feet repeatedly.

By the time the Franciscan brother behind us had picked up Mary Catherine's sippy cup for the third time and the boys had all taken five-minute turns sitting next to mom, my desire to appear holy to the other visiting pilgrims had diminished into a desire to avoid the notice of the usher, who I feared might actually kick us out. When Mary Catherine launched into a round of "Jingle Bells" as the bells were rung at the consecration, I lost it.

I leaned over to my husband, who was holding Mary Catherine, and whispered (over-loudly, he insisted later) that he take her out, recklessly unmindful of the seventeen kneeling people and one lady in a wheel chair that he would have to crawl over to exit the pew. In self-preservation mode, Mary Catherine started shouting, "Don't take me out! I sorry, Dad, I sorry!" Now the mildest of reprimands awaited her from a father who is reluctant to discipline his only little girl, but anyone nearby might have suspected we regularly beat this blond-haired angel in church parking lots.

After this display, I am ashamed to chronicle, we deteriorated even further. Back in our pew after Holy Communion, one of the younger boys gave his older brother, literally now a tabernacle of Christ, a light shove. His precarious kneeling position on the floor, as well as his instinct to make offenses seem more serious than they really are, sent him sprawling on the floor in front of God and everyone.

Every family has bad days at Mass. If it is particularly bad and lasts over an extended period of time, you can just contact the little-known branch of Catholic Charities that handles relocations and try going to Mass in a different country.

However challenging it may be at times, my husband and I believe it is worth every effort to go to Mass, especially on Sunday (which is still obligatory for Catholics, by the way). It certainly sends an unmistakable message to our children. Namely, that God deserves our worship, that we need help from God and the community to live out the Christian life, and that our authority as parents is under God's headship.

Helping children understand and participate as much as possible in the Mass has to be a deliberate choice on the part of parents and is essential in helping them get the most out of it. I have heard adults cite their own confused ideas of the Mass as one of their reasons for leaving the Catholic Church. We need to break this cycle.

Praying the Mass together is critical to family prayer life and building relationships with the God who sacrificed all so that we might live. But when children's behavior feels like a stumbling block, we need to remember why we are there and what is important. When my oldest children were small, I had somewhat militant expectations for them at Mass in reaction to a general lack of reverence sometimes displayed by others. Thankfully, an experienced mother helped me understand that Mass can be a time to treasure—to be physically close to my children and enjoy their company as we worship God together. I realized that while outward behavior in the liturgy aids greatly in authentic worship, my children will not gain heaven by folding their hands perfectly and sitting up straight in Mass.

Meditate

And when he had given thanks, he broke [the bread], and said, "This is my body which is for you. Do this in remembrance of me."

1 Corinthians 11:24

Consider

[The liturgy] is never a mere meeting of a group of people who make up their own form of celebration ... [T]hrough our sharing in Jesus' appearing before the Father, we stand both as members of the world-wide community of the whole church and also of the communion of saints. Yes, in a certain sense this is the liturgy of heaven.

Pope Benedict XVI

Pray

Loving God, knowing I will never fully understand the mystery of the Mass, I praise you for it. I want to enter more fully into the meaning and glory of this sacrifice and worship you in a way that changes me and honors you.

Day Fourteen

Works—Embracing Motherhood

Philippians 2:12 tells us to "work out [our] own salvation"—a theme found throughout Scripture. God expects us to "walk in" the good works he has prepared for us, always remembering we come into this saving relationship through faith (see Ephesians 2:8-10). Can we women accept the fact that one of the principal ways this work is accomplished in us is through childbirth and child-rearing (see 1 Timothy 2:15)? In our culture, which distorts true femininity, this reality is rejected.

Undoubtedly, there is more to life than having children and raising them, but for the married woman who is able to have children, this is the primary way for us to work out our salvation. The Catholic Church understands this so well that she requires both the man and the woman approaching the sacrament of marriage to acknowledge their intention to have children. If they are not open to having children, they cannot be validly married as Catholics. (A sacramental marriage, remember, gives us boatloads of grace, not only to be better spouses, but also better parents.)

We have to throw ourselves whole-heartedly into this motherhood thing. As a baby, my oldest son was a blond-haired, blue-eyed cherub who resembled the famed Gerber baby, only cuter. One morning, when he was only eighteen months old, this little angel approached me with a hard, narrow, plastic bat as I sat on the floor of the living room. Before I saw it coming, he brought the bat down "Whack!" on my head. I was in shock. And in the blink of an eye, *he did it again.* Coming to my senses, I made a grab for the bat and missed. My pride would not allow me to crawl away and, as unbelievable as it may sound, he wielded it deftly and clobbered me four or five times around the head and face before I could snatch the bat away.

This story reminds me of what we face as mothers. If I had caught hold of my little son and held him close, his blows would not have been able to reach me! So too, if we hold motherhood at arms' length, not really surrendering to its demands as well as its joys, we will not be able to love, or even *like*, being a mom, and we will not be allowing God to do what he wants to do in us and through us. Motherhood may even beat us black and blue.

When we do embrace motherhood, we suffer too, but it's a good kind of pain!

This is not to say that a woman is obligated to have as many children as she possibly can. There is a great responsibility that comes with parenting and "a time to embrace, and a time to refrain from embracing" (Ecclesiastes

3:5). It is essential for us to understand how to avoid having a child when necessary without *compromising the intent of the marital act*. This can be achieved through some form of natural family planning. Especially in our culture, where contraception is touted as the ultimate "freedom" fighter and pregnancy is labeled a "disease," we need to go out of our way to understand God's plan for our sexuality and fertility.

(In addition, avoiding pregnancy by natural methods has a host of measurable benefits, including the protection of women's health and the environment. This information is grossly neglected and even purposely suppressed by those who believe that sterile sex for women is an essential part of achieving equal rights with men.)

God calls us to allow motherhood to sanctify us, and our response should be thankfulness—even when part of our brain is screaming for release from the demands of motherhood. All Christians have to do "good works," which aren't always easy, but which flow from our love and gratitude to Almighty God. How merciful the Lord is to link our salvation with what most women, deep in our hearts, really desire—children.

Meditate

Women will be saved through bearing children, if she continues in faith and love and holiness, with modesty.

1 Timothy 2:15

Consider

Christ does not force our will, he only takes what we give him. But he does not give himself entirely until he sees that we yield ourselves entirely to him.

St. Teresa of Ávila

Pray

Lord, there are so many conflicting ideas about how I should regard my fertility as a woman. Help me come to know, understand, and love your perspective, believing that you have given me my body as a gift, and I can trust you to help me know its purpose.

* * * * *

Day Fifteen

Works—Evidence of Love

Bound up within this general concept of openness to life is the day-to-day, nitty-gritty "work" we do as mothers within the home, which is enough to drive us to despair by its infinite nature. Although this work is vital to our family's existence, comfort, and well-being, it makes us feel like a hamster on its wheel. Pick up the toys, so that the children have a centralized area from which to begin rapidly dispersing them. Make the dinner, and see it eaten in less than ten minutes, leaving a mess in its wake. Dress the toddler, just to change him and clean up the puddle he has made moments later. Rarely does anyone thank you for bathing them, for they are too interested in going outside and playing in the dirt. No one pays you for washing and folding their clothes, for they are too busy noticing that their favorite jeans, dutifully put in the hamper two days ago, *still* aren't clean.

If you are like me, there are days when it seems as though housework is really the sum total of existence. One day, three-year-old Dominic was naming the people in a photo that had been taken by the back door of our kitchen, "There's Patrick and Sean and Dominic and Grandpa and Mom," he said as he pointed to each person. Only when he said my name, he pointed to the colorful apron that was hanging on the wall next to the group. He thought my apron was me! Some days I do indeed feel like a walking apron. I ask myself, will there ever come a time when I will not constantly be inundated with household tasks?

The answer to this question is … yes. There will come such a time, and it will not be long before our children are either old enough to help share the load or are grown up and out of the house. I had a woman tell me just the other day that she too felt oppressed by these repetitive, mundane household tasks. Now her youngest is five and her life looks totally different than it did just a few years ago.

In the meantime, these are the daily little crosses that we can bear for the love of God and in imitation of Christ. When we do carry these little crosses with love, it gives our work more meaning and helps it become less tedious.

We can learn to do our work well and begin to take pride in it. But in all honesty, after years of trying to do my work in better, more effective ways, there are still certain chores I evade and despise. (I still avoid wiping out the refrigerator until the containers stick to the shelves and must be pried off with a butter knife.) Still, I take pride in what I can do for my family and what I have learned as a homemaker.

In the *Catechism*, various kinds of spiritual and physical service are generalized in what have traditionally been called the "Works of Mercy" (CCC, 2447). My pastor once pointed out how these works are performed by mothers and fathers hourly. After Fr. Brault pointed this out, I noticed that my husband and I engaged in about a dozen of these works during dinnertime alone!

Each duty, each hum-drum, menial task, can be used as an offering of ourselves to God, and in this way it finds additional meaning, as we not only love our family through service, but demonstrate in a most steady way our love for God. In any relationship, it is easy to *say*, "I love you," but day-in and day-out to say with our actions, "This work that I do not feel like doing, I do out of love for you"? That is truly convincing—and it is the mark of someone trying hard to grow in holiness and model God's love.

Corporal Works of Mercy

- To feed the hungry
- To give drink to the thirsty
- To clothe the naked
- To visit those in prison
- To shelter the homeless
- To visit the sick
- To bury the dead

Spiritual Works of Mercy

- To admonish the sinner
- To instruct the ignorant
- To counsel the doubtful
- To comfort the sorrowful
- To bear wrongs patiently
- To forgive all injuries
- To pray for the living and the dead

Pray

God in heaven, make me an instrument of your love, goodness, and truth to my family and to a hurting world.

Day Sixteen

Works—A Cup of Confusion

One day a delightful elderly woman knocked at my door with a basket of holiday treats for my children. I visited with her in the doorway for a few minutes, trying to block her view of the scattered rubble behind me. Since it was my most hectic time of day, with my husband about to return home from work and the children running riot, I soon thanked her and said good-bye. When I told my husband later about her visit and her generosity, he said, "Wow, that was nice of her. Did you invite her in for a cup of … confusion?"

Most families live in a state of confusion on a regular basis, but this story does highlight the value of work in a mother's day and two specific areas that need constant attention. Lack of organization in a home and undisciplined children both have the potential to destroy the peace of the entire family—and even make our homes unfit places to visit. So finding the balance in these two areas is key.

Some women find it easy to organize their homes, but for the majority of us, who struggle with it to some degree, we can glean tips and tricks from others in a few clicks of the mouse. Fifteen years ago, when I saw a program on the *Home and Garden* channel for the first time, I watched with fascination as the host, on a meager budget of $100, turned a dark, cramped closet into a multi-purpose utility room and fold-away-den. Now these kinds of shows are myriad. Homemaking, in some ways, is making a comeback, as people realize that it can be an expression of individuality, creativity, and love.

I am not naturally organized or neat, nor do I have much skill with a paintbrush or drill, but, mostly through the example of others, I have seen what a wonderful thing it is to be a homemaker and to create a place of warmth and order, a "domestic church" (CCC, 1655–1658), where loved ones and others can encounter Christ, just through visiting or sharing a meal.

When we open our homes to others, we open our hearts. We can so easily underestimate how much an invitation to our home can mean to another person—an elderly person, a lonely single person, or one of our children's friends. Maybe we can offer a listening ear to a struggling married couple or a meal to an overworked parish priest.

While this is time-consuming and perhaps a step out of our comfort zone, it is a practical way we can rise to the challenge of Pope Francis when he encourages all of us in the "art of accompaniment," in order to be the gaze of Christ to others (*Evangelii Gaudium* 169).

In the end, we need to remember the objective of keeping an orderly home: to provide a place of comfort and welcome for our families and others. Compulsive cleanliness is just as harmful to family life as disorder. Life is not just a "To Do" list; it is more of a "To Love" list, and the work we do should first and foremost be an expression of love—not primarily maintaining order so that we remain in control or feel fulfilled.

Meditate

Like the sun rising in the heights of the Lord, so is the beauty of a good wife in her well-ordered home.

Sirach 26:16

Consider

Love begins at home, and it is not how much we do ... but how much love we put in that action.

St. Teresa of Calcutta

Pray

Lord, I don't always want to do the menial tasks of homemaking or have the time or resources to make my home beautiful; please give me the grace to do my duties with love and give me the practical help I need to make a haven of my home for my family and those who visit us.

· · · · ·

Day Seventeen

Works—A Cup of Confusion, Continued

Far more destructive to familial peace than a cluttered, disorganized house is poor discipline. I was in the store snack bar one day enjoying a soft pretzel with my sons, when I overheard a mother telling her two-year-old not to roll his oversized ball onto the other side of the room. She told him again and again to stay near her, or she would take his ball away, but she never followed through. His repeated disobedience and her empty threats caused much more commotion than if she had taken his ball away and he had cried.

I realized again how imperative it is to be a good, loving disciplinarian, because in neglecting this, not only can children learn their parents don't mean what they say, but parents themselves get used to the fact that their children ignore them and stop expecting obedience! The children can hardly be blamed for the way they have been trained to respond.

It is absolutely necessary that our society care about and help children who are in abusive situations, but in an effort to treat these problems, and for other reasons, the pendulum has swung the other way and our children tend to rule the roost. Fear of "not doing it right" can also paralyze parents and keep them from doing their duty—which includes teaching their children to respect and obey them and other godly authority, to practice virtues, and to be accountable for actions.

I often see good parents who *want* to arrange their lives in a healthy way and lead their children to grow morally, spiritually, and intellectually, but they are unable to do so. They have already sabotaged themselves. They have given over so much control to their children that much of their family time is spent enduring bad behavior patiently, debating with their children, bribing them, or yelling at them. It doesn't have to deteriorate to this point!

There are reputable resources out there that can provide us with commonsense tools, but raising our children well and guiding them effectively doesn't just happen. We have to be ready to do the research and decide how we will teach and train our children, modifying our methods as needed and building healthy relationships with our kids. Keep in mind that those who claim to be experts in child-rearing are not always the ones we ought to be listening to! Experts who understand the eternal scheme of things and suggest ways to discipline with love, in imitation of God the Father, are few and far between. We should also ask advice of the parents in our lives who have well-behaved, loving children.

Perhaps the most important thing I have learned over the years is that good discipline takes an investment of time. We need to make sure we build that time into our schedules when our children are young if we want to demonstrate clearly to them our unconditional love and create a secure bond with them. Our relationship can then more readily withstand the push and pull that naturally arise between parents and children.

Time is also a vital component in the area of discipline because training children can rarely take place calmly and rationally in the middle of hectic activity. I remember working with my two-year old daughter one morning to teach her that if she threw DVDs all over the floor, she had to pick them up. It took at least an hour! There was no yelling and no spanking involved. If we do not take the time to train our children properly when they are young, what we as parents determine is best for our families will be overruled by unhappy toddlers and teenage tyrants. Then we are much more likely to fall into the trap of keeping our kids as busy as possible with extra-curricular activities or distracted by various forms of media just to keep everyone out of trouble.

Part of our indispensable work as mothers is to make every effort to arrange our lives in a way that lends itself to order and harmony. Family life may often be a circus, but we can still be good ringmasters!

Meditate

The rod and reproof give wisdom, but a child left to himself brings shame to his mother.

Proverbs 29:15

Consider

Having a family is like having a bowling alley installed in your head.

Martin Mull

Pray

Dear God, I praise you. You know how difficult it is for me sometimes to discern how to discipline my children. Help me learn how to do this better and give me the strength not to give up or wait until a more "convenient" time. Help me and my children recognize the fact that proper discipline is an act of immense love.

* * * * *

Day Eighteen

Joy—The Natural Result of the "Little Way"

Joy is a natural result of the "little way of motherhood." Think of the "work" we discussed over the past four days. *Tasks well done* bring order and good fruit from our lives, which leads to joy even on a natural level—how much more so when we do our duties for the love of God!

We have also talked a great deal about *living virtuously*, which brings order and good fruit from our lives, as well. When we choose to follow God's commandments and strive to follow God's will, there is no doubt that we get better results, even with life's curve balls. Practicing patience, following God's plan for our sexuality, forgiveness, self-discipline, and all of the other virtues lead to peace and harmony with ourselves and others and become a great source of joy. It is hard to imagine, for instance, the joy a loving couple must feel when they celebrate their fiftieth wedding anniversary—

when they have spent fifty years treating each other in a Christian manner and living virtuous lives.

We have also devoted several of our daily reflections to prayer, which takes us right inside God's heart. As we build *intimacy with God,* based in prayer and a habit of listening for God's voice and direction, we begin to experience the kind of joy that the world cannot understand—a joy that the saints often experienced and which we can all participate in to some degree on our faith journeys.

We ought to pause and ask ourselves if we have the joy that flows from intimacy with God. Have we ever reached for our Bible with the same enthusiasm as we reach for a box of chocolates? Do we sometimes hear God's voice so clearly that we laugh out loud from the sheer joy of knowing he cares? If not, we need to seek friendship with God more actively.

Sometimes intimacy with God is felt most deeply after we experience significant trials in our lives. First comes the obedience and trust, sometimes involving great sacrifice and even a feeling of abandonment or dryness in our prayer, then comes the joy in perceiving how God was with us through those difficult times and helping us all along. I can think of many stories from my own life that continue to bring me joy and consolation years after they took place. I will share an example of God's faithfulness in the area of family finances which friends of mine experienced.

Christine and Marques had four small children. They lived in one of the most expensive parts of Virginia, barely making ends meet month after month. As a couple, they had always been radically committed to doing God's will above all else, but when Marques lost his job and couldn't find another, they became desperate to the point of actual empty cupboards.

One evening, as Christine scrounged around her kitchen trying to find enough food with which to make supper, she cried aloud in desperation, "Lord, we have no meat!" Soon afterward there was a knock on the door. On the doorstep was a delivery that had been sent as a gift from Marques' aunt—a cooler from the Omaha Steak Company containing steaks and ground beef!

Living a life of dependence on God gives him the opportunity to demonstrate his love for us in ordinary and sometimes extraordinary ways and this becomes a source of profound joy.

Nothing compares with the joy of living in friendship with God and the deep satisfaction of knowing that he is our loving Father. This joyful assurance is mightily strengthened when we try our best to do our duty, live virtuously, and develop an intimate relationship with God through prayer and radical trust.

Meditate

"If you keep my commandments, you will abide in my love ... These things I have spoken to you, that my joy may be in you, and that your joy may be full."

John 15:10-11

Consider

Christian joy is a gift of God flowing from a good conscience.

St. Philip Neri

Pray

Jesus, you pleased your Heavenly Father perfectly. Help us follow your example, to live holy lives and to develop an intimacy with God, so that our "joy may be full."

* * * * *

Day Nineteen

Joy—Be Grateful

There are two more aspects of joy I want to talk about over the next two days. Today, let's think about how we can find more enjoyment in our family lives—to foster moments of joy in our day and to thank God for these moments.

In the Morning Offering, you may remember, we offer God our "joys" as well as our prayers, works, sorrows, and sufferings. These "joys" are often moments of enjoyment or pleasure that arise quite naturally. When we enjoy our family life more, it makes us better mothers. We want to be with our children, and we are strengthened to meet their needs. We can offer these moments to God with heartfelt gratitude, and gratitude to God leads to more joy!

It is clear that there are many occasions of joy in a mother's life if only we recognize them. At the start of our mothering experience, pregnancy, even when it is difficult, has its delightful and miraculous aspects. These are God's gifts to us which we can completely miss if we are busy whining about the trials often associated with pregnancy. The privilege of nurturing and guarding a child in the womb, and the pride in participating in God's deliberate plan to create another human being, are meant to be enjoyed.

Spousal and sibling excitement doubles the joy. I remember one pregnancy when four-year-old Sean wrapped his arms around my huge midsection and said with an endearing grin, "I love the baby. It's a beautiful tummy-of-a-baby." The eager participation of my older children in planning for a new baby is a poignant reminder of the way love multiplies. These are the aspects of pregnancy that we should be calling to mind instead of focusing on the negative.

Personally speaking, as my children have grown and are no longer cute little babies, I can easily become too focused on what needs to be corrected or "fixed" in them. I have to make an effort to curb this tendency, otherwise I'll become too stressed-out to give my children a chance to show me a side of themselves that I can enjoy—and they certainly do not see me at my best either. Children can be hilarious, and the situations in which we find ourselves when we hang around with them are no less so. If we let ourselves just laugh when is appropriate to laugh, it can be such a victory over ourselves and our fallen human nature.

There was a day that I was frustrated with my three-year-old, who was not listening to me and who more often than not, had his head in the clouds. Desperately struggling not to raise my voice as I attempted to get my kids ready to leave the house, I demanded in a loud sing-song monotone, "Sean-get-your-boots-from-your-room-right-now!" Four-year-old Patrick solemnly intoned, "A-men!" It would be a sin not to laugh.

On another occasion, when my children were quite a bit older, they were bickering and misbehaving for hours, and I found myself ready to explode. While holding my toddler, I attempted to relieve my tension by kicking a large empty box in my most impressive ex-soccer player style. Surely this display of power, combined with the manic look in my eye, would communicate to them that Mom meant business! Unfortunately, my foot went through the box and the box became stuck on my foot. I lurched and reeled about trying to regain my footing, toddler in my arms! A choice was placed before me: I could become even more outraged or I could laugh. I made the wise choice, let my pride go, and allowed myself to laugh. Interestingly enough, the incident provided the necessary diversion to change the overall atmosphere, and the children's behavior and my outlook took a positive turn.

Years later, the joy of those memories and many others, continue to bring a smile to my face. When all of the pain, difficulties, and stress of parenting young children are over, these moments are the ones that stay with us and continue to give us joy.

Limiting constraints on our time and attention is also a major factor in helping us appreciate our children and enjoy being with them. I don't think this point can be emphasized enough. We will not learn to enjoy our family life if we do not embrace family life here and now—making it our top priority to meet the needs of our spouse and children. To learn who our children are and what makes them tick, we have to be intentional about our behaviors and ask ourselves questions like: What have I picked up more often today, my baby or my smartphone? Do I really listen to my daughter when she is speaking to me, or am I on mommy auto-pilot? Do I smile and make eye contact with strangers or acquaintances more often than I smile at my family members?

How sad it is, and how many opportunities we lose of enjoying our family life, when we fail to focus on the present moment—when we fail to engage with the people right in front of us.

Sometimes the demands that parenthood places on us cause us to forget how much joy there is in our daily lives, especially if our personalities aren't naturally optimistic or cheerful. Good, beautiful, creative, inspiring, marvelous things are all around us, in creation, in our fellow human beings, and, most assuredly, in our families. Let's find these occasions of joy, foster them, and thank God for them!

Meditate

Oh sing to the Lord a new song, for he has done marvelous things!

Psalm 98:1

Consider

We pray for the big things and forget to give thanks for the ordinary, small (and yet really not small) gifts.

Dietrich Bonhoeffer

Pray

Oh God, the God of joy, let this fruit of the Holy Spirit be more fully released in my life and open my eyes to your goodness everywhere. I thank and praise you for the gift of humor, laughter, and fun, especially in my family!

Day Twenty

Joy—Choose It or Lose It

Mothers who are living in the midst of less-than-ideal circumstances can still find ways to enjoy life, but there is no denying that it takes effort. For a period of years in my life as a mother, I became depressed and anxious as a number of fairly serious problems assaulted our family. Heroism was not my goal ... just getting through the day was.

I remember coming to the realization that I hated my life and making a determined effort to enjoy each good moment, though I knew it would be opposed to my feelings. One time in particular, I was hanging clothes on the line and I said to myself, "I am going to enjoy hanging out these clothes!" With a deep breath and a spirit of determination, I took a pair of wet jeans from the laundry basket and energetically shook them out. As I did so, a dime flew out of one of the pockets and sharply flicked me on the cheek, surprising me into tears. It was like Satan, who is the father of lies, was telling me, "Face it ... your life sucks!" The evil one did not want me choosing joy. When we persevere in choosing to be joyful, even if it is done imperfectly, we win a victory over ourselves and the evil one.

Thankfully, those distressing circumstances in my life were eventually resolved, but I have always had somewhat of a melancholic temperament, and it isn't always easy to be joyful or thankful.

One day I heard a woman on Christian radio who was funny, inspiring, and unmistakably joyful. She was sharing that when she was a girl, her alcoholic father would come home at night plastered and profane, but her mother, a believer, managed to instill in her daughter an optimistic attitude. Every morning this mother would wake her daughter with words like, "Good morning, darling! It's going to be a beautiful day! I wonder what God is going to do for us today? What can we do for him?"

As I have already indicated, the early morning does not find me at my best. As a young woman dreaming of a husband and children, I was idealistic about what family life would entail. I didn't anticipate the reality of climbing out of a warm, friendly bed to deal immediately with a misplaced homework folder, a fussy four-year-old who is shivering with cold because he refuses to dress himself, a child who "hates oatmeal," and the dreaded feeling that the baby is coming down with another cold. All of this and more before seven a.m.! My attitude, especially for the first fifteen minutes of the day, can be, "What's the use in living?" Over the next half hour it graduates slightly to, "I guess I'll go on for another day."

The words that I heard this woman speak on the radio touched me as I thought about the power that I have to help my children "choose" joy by choosing it myself, no matter what my circumstances are. Starting each morning with a positive attitude seemed a logical place to start. I resolved to try it, though for upbeat words to come out of my mouth only minutes after waking up seemed like spreading jam on the insole of an old shoe.

The next morning it was particularly hard to get out of bed. My husband woke me by wrapping his arms around me and holding me close for a moment. I remained unmoved and immovable. One refrain ran through my head, "Sleep come back! Sleep come back!" Aloud I whined, "Can't I sleep until 6:40?" Pat got out of bed and said with matter-of-fact cruelty, "It's 6:41."

Downstairs, as we all went about our morning business, I worked up a fraction of enthusiasm. I was going to start *today* to live in the joy of the Lord. I said brightly, "It's going to be a beautiful day!" Three of the boys kept slurping down cereal, but Patrick Jr. looked up for a moment to say, "If it doesn't rain."

"It will still be a beautiful day," I answered, determined. Patrick tossed his empty cereal bowl into the sink and said, "What's up with you?" as he left the room to go brush his teeth. He recognizes jam on old insole when he sees it.

I have learned by experience that we can "choose joy" in ways that don't try to rewrite our own personalities but will, nevertheless, combat melancholic tendencies. We can be taking good care of our families in so many ways, but if they know we are just doing our duty without any real joy in our lives, they may soon wonder if serving Christ is worth it.

The fact is, the more we grow in our relationship with God and learn to love others unconditionally, the more we will see even the sacrifices we make as occasions of joy. To a saint who has reached perfection by God's grace, *everything is joy*.

Meditate

Count it all joy, my brethren, when you meet various trials, for you know that the testing of your faith produces steadfastness. And let steadfastness have its full effect, that you may be perfect and complete, lacking in nothing.

James 1:2-4

Consider

Be merry, really merry. The life of a true Christian should be a perpetual jubilee, a prelude to the festivals of eternity.

St. Theophane Venard

Pray

No matter what the circumstances, Lord God, I want to live joyfully, knowing that you are the source of every good thing and that you share your riches with me.

· · · · ·

Day Twenty-One

Sorrows and Sufferings— Little Things Add Up

Suffering is one of the most important topics we will discuss in this twenty-eight-day-series of reflections. This is the area in which our faith can really be tested, and we have to try to understand the role that suffering plays in our lives in order to be steadfast when those tests come.

Because we are human beings, we are made to know, love, and serve God *in our bodies.* Our soul is linked with our bodies in a way that the angels do not experience, and this gives us a great capacity for suffering in various ways and degrees.

Suffering is a natural result of "the fall" of mankind. Thankfully, the life and death of Jesus redeems the fallen and imperfect. If we want to understand suffering, we look primarily to Our Lord's suffering. It is helpful to keep his passion in mind as we canvass the topic of "sorrows and sufferings" over the next three days. I would urge you to take out a crucifix and place it in front of you as you think about this topic.

Before we discuss the serious and intense ways mothers can suffer, I would like to comment on small "s" sufferings, which are very much a part of everyday heroism and something we have touched on in previous reflections. For these, there is a common Catholic phrase that may sound familiar: "Offer it up."

Hearing this phrase uttered glibly or frequently can warp its meaning, but it is a particularly profound concept when discussing "sorrows and sufferings." In one of his papal letters—Pope Benedict XVI addressed this practice:

> There used to be a form of devotion—perhaps less practiced today but quite widespread not long ago—that included the idea of "offering up" the minor daily hardships that continually strike at us like irritating "jabs," thereby giving them a meaning ... What does it mean to offer something up? Those who did so were convinced that they could insert these little annoyances into Christ's great "com-passion" so that they somehow became part of the treasury of compassion so greatly needed by the human race (*Spe Salvi* 40).

I once shared an analogy with my children that highlights the frequency and effect of these "jabs." I called a family meeting one day when my kids were driving me crazy, and I told them this little story.

"Imagine you have been looking forward to visiting an amusement park for a long time. You have heard what a great place it is, and you are finally going. Even better, you are taking along your two BFs. When you get to the amusement park, you go on a few rides and visit the various attractions. Sure enough, this place is awesome!

Something keeps happening, though, as you walk from place to place with your best friends, chatting and joking and having (mostly) a great time: The crowds tend to jostle you and a few people even elbow you in the ribs. Several times someone gives you a hard pinch. But what really bothers you is that your friends start doing it too. Suddenly, one of them pokes you in the eye ... seemingly on purpose! Worst of all, at one point, one of your friends trips your other friend and kicks him in the gut while he is down. You desperately want to enjoy yourself, but you can't fully do so under these conditions. It is physically painful, but even more so, it causes emotional tension and strain."

I explained to my crew of young people how this story was analogous to our family life. I assured them that I have looked forward to being a mom for as long as I can remember. Even though sometimes my job required a measure of sacrifice (the jostling of the crowd), there is nowhere else in the world I would rather be. The hard part, I told them, was being poorly treated by my dear children and even more so, seeing them mistreat each other.

I told my kids this story with the hope that it would change their behavior. It deeply impressed them and transformed our family life. Just kidding.

Truth be told, the daily pokes, prods, and tensions of our otherwise delightful adventure of motherhood can really be a drag. They are a Chinese-water-torture-kind-of-thing. But let's remember to offer them up. For, thankfully, our Catholic tradition reminds us that these annoyances and stresses are invaluable in helping us become who we are called by Christ to be, burning away selfishness and pride (if we let them), and giving our prayer additional power.

One small suffering I had problems with, especially when my children were younger, was boredom. I am not a person who is particularly suited to the care of preschool or young children. As adorable as they are, there seems to be an inordinate amount of time spent reviewing colors and numbers, reading the same book multiple times, admiring Lego towers, and, my personal least favorite activity of all time, playing with mutilated dolls in ill-fitting dresses.

One day I was watching my children on the playground, and they called me over to observe all of their remarkable feats. I pretended to be amazed as I yawned and yawned, until I realized tears were dripping down my face. I was literally bored to tears. Thinking of this incident, I recall Psalm 56 in which David remarks that his tears (of sorrow) are stored in God's flask and remembered by him. I think tears of boredom are noted by God in a special way too, if, out of love for him, we carefully carry out the tasks we find most tedious and offer this sacrifice to him.

As our children got older, I found new things to "offer up." Regardless of the fact that I've always looked forward to my children becoming teens, I've been dismayed by the occasional adolescent glower or the "that is the stupidest thing I've ever heard" smirk. Annoying behavior, goofing-off, tattling, and bickering are intensified just as I feel my children ought to be maturing. I find myself having to battle for self-control.

I remember a day at Mass in which I was harboring a grudge toward one of my sons. He was creating a great deal of stress in my life, especially through his interaction with his brothers. When the Gospel reading from Luke said, "... love your enemies ... pray for those who mistreat you," I started crying—it is not pleasant to realize your own child is the enemy!

When we choose to offer up our daily trials, we "die to self," and this effort does not go unseen by God or unrewarded.

Meditate

But if we have died with Christ, we believe that we shall also live with him.

Romans 6:8

Consider

Do as the storekeeper does with his merchandise; make a profit on every article. Suffer not the loss of the tiniest fragment of the true cross. It may only be the sting of a fly or the point of a pin that annoys you; it may be the little eccentricities of a neighbor, some unintentional slight, the insignificant loss of a penny, some little restlessness of soul, a light pain in your limbs. Make a profit on every article as the grocer does, and you will soon be wealthy in God.

St. Louis Marie de Montfort

Pray

Dear Jesus, I want to make use of every little irritation, pain, and disappointment. Help me recognize the power in offering up these daily trials, a practice which not only helps me die to myself, but makes me truly alive in you and able to intercede effectively for the needs of others.

Day Twenty-Two

Sorrows and Sufferings— When it Really Hurts

There are many levels of suffering. Perhaps we can call this next level medium "s" sufferings—encompassing that pain which is unlike almost anything we have experienced before, but at the same time isn't unexpected or "unbearable." (It is difficult to categorize suffering! This level covers a particularly wide gamut. Plus, what might be only very painful for some might be considered "unbearable" to others.)

Usually pregnancy and childbirth, or the difficulties associated with adoption, are the first ways a mother really starts to wake up to the idea that motherhood demands sacrifice on a whole new level. One of the obvious ways that a biological mother suffers is through what she encounters by allowing her body to bring about and support new life, even amidst the potential joys of pregnancy. We are on the highway of procreation with no exits or rest areas for the next nine months. Beyond the nausea, the fatigue, and the innumerable other discomforts of pregnancy, we can be faced with debilitating problems.

My fifth pregnancy particularly challenged me. The first two months of nausea were so intense that I felt panicked by my inability to cope, especially with four young boys to care for. One day, after passing by the washer and dryer several times, I started frantically rummaging around on some of the shelves. Sure enough, there were several bars of strong-smelling soap wrapped in plastic bags. They had been in the bathroom, and since their odor had been nauseating me, I had told my husband to get rid of them. "They go, or I go!" I had snarled, albeit weakly, from the couch. Now I hurled the twice-despised bricks of soap violently out the back door, thinking, "Does he think I'm making this stuff up?"

There are times when all we can do is struggle against our feelings of despair, as we beg for the grace and mercy to make it through. God appreciates the very fact that we continue putting one foot in front of the other for his sake, and he brings fruit from our exertions.

Beyond the physical problems, there are also other sufferings associated with pregnancy. One hundred years ago, men and women knew that if they had sex, they might have a baby. Not so today. Young women fall victim to this unscientific and unreasonable disconnect between sex and babies, leading to many unexpected pregnancies. Dangerous pregnancies can also cause great mental and emotional suffering.

Then there are women who cannot bear children of their own and experience not only the pain of infertility, which can be agonizing, but if they adopt children, open themselves to the possibility of suffering in other ways. Alice and her husband Ben adopted a little girl from India when she was very young. Alice shares:

> Our daughter struggled with the effects of having had no mother during her first years. She had difficulty allowing us to take care of her. As a baby she learned that there was no one to do it ... and she became as self-sufficient as possible.
>
> Every day I grieve over the suffering my daughter experienced and of which there will always be a shadow in her beautiful, dark eyes. It often makes me catch my breath and stop — a visual reminder to be gentler, more patient, and grateful for what my daughter and I are to each other now.

Another kind of suffering that can escalate and become very serious is depression or some sort of mental or emotional hurdle. Exacerbated by hormone fluctuations associated with bearing children, tendencies toward depression and anxiety can worsen. The intense care and concern we mothers have for our children's well-being can morbidly prey on our minds if our thinking and reasoning isn't healthy. Some of my greatest suffering as a mom has been over issues that no one else can perceive, especially concerning fears about my children. These nearly obsessive thoughts certainly had their foundations in reality, but when I was suffering from periods of anxiety and depression, they were blown all out of proportion.

The determination to offer everything to God, *especially* when we feel he is not present to us, is truly heroic. Jesus experienced this feeling during his passion and he continued trusting the Father. In his mercy, Jesus then sent us the Holy Spirit, so that we would have the strength to live the life he is calling us to. He also gave us the sacraments, which are a sure well-spring of abundant graces. This grace empowers us to unite our sufferings with the sufferings of Jesus and to cooperate in his mission to save the world.

The concept of participating in the sufferings of Christ in order to bring others to salvation is not well understood by Christians, but it is biblical and has long been supported by Christian practice. Meditate on the following Scripture verse as you think about this life-changing reality, and we will reflect on it again tomorrow.

Meditate

Now I rejoice in my sufferings for your sake, and in my flesh I complete what is lacking in Christ's afflictions for the sake of his body, that is, the church.

Colossians 1:24

Consider

In light of heaven, the worst suffering on earth will be seen to be no more serious than one night in an inconvenient hotel.

St. Teresa of Ávila

Pray

Life hurts sometimes, Lord, and it is so easy to question why. Give me the faith I need to know that you bring beauty from ashes and to continue trusting in your omniscient goodness.

* * * * *

Day Twenty-Three

Sorrows and Sufferings—On the Cross

At the pinnacle of suffering, human experience shows us repeatedly that mothers can suffer so tragically and heart-wrenchingly that it hurts to even look upon their pain.

Martha, a family friend, told me a story about their oldest child, Paul, who was always a bit rebellious and who, in his early twenties, drank too much and smoked marijuana. His life was unfocused and drifting. Martha, a faithful Catholic woman, agonized over her son for years, fearing for his soul, knowing he was living life on the edge. It was a dark and distressing time. One day, with radical faithfulness, she gave the Blessed Mother permission to do *whatever it took* in order to bring Paul back into a life of grace.

The next day, early in the morning, she and her husband received a phone call telling them that Paul was in shock trauma at the hospital. Driving while intoxicated, he had broken his neck in a car accident. He suffered physically and mentally on the road to recovery, as did his parents, but over a period of time he experienced deep conversion. Several years later he announced his intentions to enter the priesthood. Martha lovingly calls the Blessed Mother "Momma Mafia Mary" ("I breaka you neck!").

Some stories of terrible suffering don't resolve into a happy ending. At least not this side of heaven. I was pregnant with my daughter when I received the call about Brittany and Bionca. They were my cousin Ann's daughters, fourteen and fifteen years old respectively, and they were beautiful, bubbly Southern girls. (The year before, we had visited them in Tennessee, and they had embraced us enthusiastically at the door, though they hardly knew us, and had taken our little boys under their care, making quite an impression on us!)

During this phone call, I learned that Brittany and Bionca had decided to drive home with a friend from school instead of taking the bus. The car had a full tank of gas, and when it hit a culvert ... there was no time to rescue them before the car went up in flames. All I could think of was their mother, Ann. What happened to her heart that day?

In the Blessed Mother, God has given us a model of the suffering mother. In her story, I find assurance that God's ways are higher than our ways and embrace the conviction that we can trust our Heavenly Father, even in the darkest of times.

As I watched the movie *The Passion of the Christ* for the first time, although I certainly found myself overwhelmed by the agonies that Christ voluntarily endured for my sake, I was largely unprepared for the anguish of his mother, which I felt to the core of my maternal being. I had already been weeping steadily, but at the point in which our Blessed Mother greets Jesus on the way to Calvary and remembers him as a child, I sobbed uncontrollably.

Thinking that the pain we can experience as mothers serves no purpose is a grave mistake. Jesus could have protected his own beloved Mother from all of the pain she experienced. He could have asked his Father to take her to heaven beforehand, or even asked the disciple, John, to conceal from her what was happening. How telling it is that Jesus allowed his mother to walk the way of the cross with him. He knew that her suffering—and the suffering of all the faithful across the ages—could be united to his own with such far-reaching benefits for mankind that it can never be fully comprehended this side of heaven.

Meditate

Then [Jesus] said to them, "My soul is very sorrowful, even to death ..." And going a little farther he fell on his face and prayed, "My Father, if it be possible, let this chalice pass from me; nevertheless, not as I will, but as you will."

Matthew 26:38-39

Consider

I know that these contradictory events are permitted and guided by thy wisdom, which solely is light. We are in darkness and must be thankful that our knowledge is not wanted [needed] to perfect thy work.

St. Elizabeth Anne Seton

Pray

Dear Blessed Mother, you whose "yes" to God enabled Jesus to take on flesh and fulfill the will of the Father, pray for me during times of great trial, that I will choose to do the will of the Father. Please comfort me with your maternal love.

. . . . .

Day Twenty-Four

Setting the World Ablaze

Once we have surrendered our lives to God and begin to live out the "little way of motherhood" in our daily duties—offering God all of our prayers, works, joys, sorrows, and sufferings—our lives take on purpose and meaning. Ideally, we grow in an internal awareness that the challenges and messiness of family life, while they still may bring us to tears at times, can be life-changing. If we let him, God can form us and shape us into heroic, saintly women whose lives forever alter the course of history.

St. Catherine of Siena said it this way: "If you are what you should be, you will set the world ablaze." I love that image.

When we learn to make our lives an offering to God, everything from the drudgery to the very act of being a life-giver to all of our fears and joys, he takes this seemingly insignificant and imperfect offering and uses it as kindling. Igniting us with his own flame, he breathes on us … and sets the world ablaze.

But even when we don't see the results of offering everything to God, we must believe in the words of Sacred Scripture, which tells us that "all things work for good for those who love God who are called according to his purpose" (see Romans 8:28). Facing the fact that while on this earth, we may *never* see the luminous glow of the blaze that starts with our obedience to God, we must continue to offer Christ our lives as kindling. The fiery result of our faithfulness is ultimately God's business.

As we ponder today's quotation, let's allow the words of Fr. Thomas Dubay to confirm in us that God is busy using us to set the world ablaze!

Meditate

"I came to cast fire on the earth; and would that it were already kindled!"

Luke 12:49

Consider

In our day the divine fire has not been extinguished ... The proven *incapacity* of committees and clubs, speeches and surveys, electronics and entertainment profoundly and permanently to change vast numbers of people for the better has to be conceded. As the experience of the centuries attests, true transformations in the world and in the Church continue to come about only through the interventions of men and women on fire—that is, through saints.

Fr. Thomas Dubay

Pray

Dear Heavenly Father, breathe on me with the fire of the Holy Spirit, make me what I should be and, through me, set the world ablaze.

PART III

Teenagers, Education, and Mission

I can do all things in him who strengthens me.

Philippians 4:13

Day Twenty-Five

The Teen Years

I will use the last few reflections in this book to talk about some miscellaneous items that are so essential to our vocation as mothers and everyday heroes that I dare not leave them out!

The teen years. Let me start by saying there are things I love about these years. As a teacher and a catechist, this is my favorite age-group to work with. Nevertheless, about the time my oldest son entered junior high, I started saying to myself with increased frequency, "Mmmm … this is very interesting …" It is a phrase I often use when I am trying not to curse.

As new parents, my husband and I put a lot of thought into how we might raise our children in a way that would make the years of transition from childhood into adulthood go smoothly. Right from the beginning, we worked at it and planned for it.

Was all of this hard work worth it? Did it make the teen years easier? Yes.

Have the teen years perplexed and rattled us despite our best efforts? Heck yeah!

I remember the moment when I realized our oldest son was no longer a child. Wrestling among brothers has always been the norm in our family and often involves Dad as well. One morning, I was in our bedroom putting away clothes when I heard scuffling in the hall just outside our room. I offered my usual caution, "Be careful! Someone-is-going-to-get-hurt ..." Moments passed and things quieted down. I could hear some brief conversation between our oldest son, then fourteen, and my husband. Soon, Pat came strolling into the bedroom and then quickly sort of hid himself behind the door, so that I was the only one who could see him. His nonchalant attitude vanished as he gripped his left wrist. Grimacing, he mouthed the words, "He hurt me!"

In many ways, we spent the next four years grappling with this man-child. Patrick was a good boy, but he was growing up and asserting his independence, and sometimes he resented us for thwarting him. We sometimes resented him for making our lives difficult. He went away to college in a different state when he was eighteen, and things took a turn for the better in our relationship. (It's not that I didn't cry when he went away, I just didn't cry *much*.) Of course, we still had two other teenagers in the house at the time, so we weren't off the hook.

Since then, we have navigated the teen years with most of our children. As unique as each child was, we had similar growing pains with each one. While my kids were punching holes in the walls and jumping out of windows to escape our tyrannical parenting methods, I was kicking furniture and spouting sarcasm to combat their general idiocy. It got pretty ugly at times, and I am not proud of it.

Then there is the anxiety. There is so much to worry about when they are teenagers! Why don't they have more friends? When will they ever find their niche? Are they *too* popular for their own good? Are they safe drivers? What are they looking at and listening to on their phones? And my all-time favorite as a Catholic mom: When you ask your son why he wasn't home when you told him to be and he says, "I stopped at the church to go to confession," can you believe him?

Ultimately, especially in our culture, the years between childhood and adulthood can be tricky, but laying a strong foundational relationship with our children when they were young has been crucial to whatever success my husband and I have experienced. If you still have young children, spend oodles of time with them! One day you will wake up and you will have teens who will find it hard to relate to you. All of the work you have put into making yourselves a vital part of their lives can carry you through this rough patch.

Another thing to remember as a parent of teens may seem obvious, but it is easy to forget: We must not give up parenting our adolescent children. They still need us to parent them, just not in the same way as when they were little. Our older children need reasonable rules, household responsibilities, and accountability. They also need a lot of attention, touch, and affirmation. There are experts who can help Catholics navigate these issues!

Finally, we parents have to be *serious* about praying for our children. In the end, they will be making their own life choices, and they need grace to help them make good ones!

God made this need for prayer clear to me one night when I woke up in a cold sweat, panicking about one of my older teenagers who was in his first year of college and who seemed to be floundering. Always a good sleeper, I had started waking up this way with increased frequency. On this occasion, I was paralyzed with fear and couldn't even pray. My husband woke up and started praying out loud.

Desperate for a word from God, I opened my Bible just as my husband began interceding for our children by name. Immediately, my eyes fell upon these words, "Arise, cry out in the night, at the beginning of the watches! Pour out your heart like water before the presence of the Lord! Lift your hands to him for the lives of your children, who faint for hunger at the head of every street" (Lamentations 2:19).

In this case, I knew that my child was experiencing the kind of hunger referred to in Amos 8:11-13, a famine not of bread and water, but a spiritual famine—a by-product of living in a society that does not encourage young people to seek a relationship with God or follow his commandments.

I don't know what good came of praying for my son that night, but he made it through that tumultuous period of his life, and I believe our on-going prayers played a key role in protecting him and strengthening him. I also believe that God used the circumstances of that night to impress upon my husband and me how vital it is to pray for all of our children frequently and with fervor.

The "hunger" young people experience in our present cultural atmosphere is a spiritual one, and our children are in need of our *sacrificial* intercession. We must pray, fast, and sacrifice for them, so that they receive the graces they need to find their way.

Meditate

"Behold, the days are coming," says the Lord God, "when I will send a famine on the land; not a famine of bread, nor a thirst for water, but of hearing the words of the Lord. They shall wander from sea to sea and from north to east; they shall run back and forth, to seek the word of the Lord, but they shall not find it. In that day the fair virgins and the young men shall faint for thirst ..."

Amos 8:11-13

Consider

Teenagers: Tired of being harassed by your parents? ACT NOW!! Move out, get a job, pay your own way. While you still know everything!!

Pray

Jesus, you were an adolescent once ... please give me the wisdom and insight to understand what my child is thinking and experiencing as they transition from childhood into adulthood. Help me guide him/her properly and to meet his/her needs. Help me to never give up on my duties and responsibilities as a parent and to demonstrate to my child unconditional love at all times. Thank you for the gift of my teenager!

Day Twenty-Six

Taking the Wheel

The second topic I want to cover as we approach the end of our journey together deserves our utmost attention: our children's education. As many experts admit, the educational system in our country is problematic, to say the least. The state will never be able to fix our problems in this area because it is not primarily their job. It's ours! How many parents have forgotten or have never been taught that it is *their* right and responsibility to be the primary educators of their children (CCC 2223)?

One day, I went in to our local public school to talk to a teacher about the book list she had chosen for my son's English curriculum. I was horrified by some of the content and deeply concerned about the unilateral trust placed in the school system to use this material without involving parents. Even more disturbing was the silence and lack of concern on the part of most of the other parents. Thankfully, when

I approached my son's teacher, she was kind and willing to listen.

One of the things my son's teacher and I agreed upon is the necessity of discussing moral, theological, and philosophical subjects with students as they mature. Naturally, I pointed out how the information they receive about these topics and the tone of such discussions are often not compatible with the Catholic worldview. I went on to state that most parents don't have a fraction of the time that a school teacher has to discuss these sensitive issues with their child and that the educational system should help facilitate the parent–child connection, not usurp it. (She seemed to agree, perhaps because she is a parent herself.)

If, as Catholic parents, we don't do something drastically different from what "everyone else is doing," we cannot hope to fulfill our obligation to be the primary educators of our children. We simply won't get enough access to them.

Over the past fifty years, the values of our society have changed so radically, we parents are compelled to respond radically when it comes to educating our children. We must be creative and diligent in this area, while we have the chance.

For my husband and me, this creativity has necessitated a mixture of Catholic school, homeschooling, and public school, with a brief stint in a non-denominational Christian school. Sounds complicated, and in a way it has been. Ironically, in order to live simply, sometimes things do get complicated! And I have yet to see two good Catholic families do it exactly the same way.

In making educational choices for our children, we started with the deliberate decision to put first things first. We knew it was our job to make sure that things of eternal value stay at the top of the list—something that doesn't "just happen." Relationships with God and each other take priority, but general education, service to others, friendship building, and opportunities for recreation all had a vital place in raising well-rounded individuals who could function in a post-Christian culture.

I am not going to lie ... taking charge of our children's education in this way has been a challenge. Nevertheless, while the effort, prayer, and dare I say risk, that has gone into maintaining our priorities has been the primary work of our lives, it has also been the most satisfying. We have watched in awe at the fruit that has come from the radical, though woefully imperfect, efforts we have made.

In particular, when it comes to educating children, it is important that we find ways to help them see that the Catholic Faith isn't just another subject. On the contrary, it provides a context for everything else we learn.

I have heard it said that faith is "caught, not taught," and in a certain context, this is true. In another, practical context, however, faith needs to be taught *in order to be* caught. If our children do not understand that Jesus was a historical person, for example, or that for thousands of years people have lived and died convinced, through the use of their intellect and experience, of the truths taught by the Catholic Church, they will not respect the faith enough to embrace it for themselves. By sixth grade it is seen as irrelevant, by ninth grade it is slightly ridiculous and by college-age, young adults who have not been well-taught cannot give even one reasonable answer for why they believe. Often any vestige of faith is driven out of them by aggressive secularists and atheists found in abundance in the collegiate setting.

Furthermore, children need to be guided in prayer. They need to know how to access God. How to access grace. How to start over when they have failed. Children need a personal relationship with God and opportunities to see his love and power in action. Practicing *lectio divina* as a family, making frequent confession a priority, praying over our children, and sending them to dynamic youth conferences are a few ways that we can foster our children's personal relationship with God.

All around us we see parents, as loving and as well-intentioned as they may be, more concerned about what sports their children are involved in than whether or not their child knows what it takes to live their lives well and to reach heaven. Often we parents who know better, fall into this trap as well, thinking that when it comes to educating our children, we must take a back seat to teachers, coaches, and internet sources. It can be daunting to act in opposition to this mentality, but God wants to give us all the graces necessary to do what we are called to do. We must realize that it is our responsibility to "take the wheel," if we want to have any control of our families' final destination.

Meditate

Parents must be acknowledged as the first and foremost educators of their children. Their role as educators is so decisive that scarcely anything can compensate for their failure in it.

Declaration on Christian Education

Consider

Every education teaches a philosophy, if not by dogma, then by suggestion, by implication, by atmosphere. Every part of that education has a connection with every other part. If it does not all combine to convey some general view of life, it is not education at all.

G.K. Chesterton

Pray

God, show [my husband and me] the way to be faithful in our [my]role as our [my] child(ren)'s primary educator[s]. Give us[me] the grace and the practical helps we [I] need to "take the wheel."

* * * * *

Day Twenty-Seven

Messy, Mysterious, and Entrusted with a Mission

Before speaking about the mission of the Catholic family in the modern world, I'd like to recognize some tough realities. Family life is messy and mysterious at the best of times, and many families are fractured in some way. The ideal situation is for a person to enter into matrimony already a mature Christian, prepared in practical ways to be a loving spouse and wise parent. But often we are still growing up ourselves when we enter marriage, or we have not yet experienced personal conversion, or our past has not provided us with the tools and guidance we need. Life barrels on as we play "catch-up." Some women become mothers without ever having the advantage of marriage and others find themselves married to men whose immaturity or woundedness are largely responsible for fracturing the unity of the family, either through divorce or in some other way.

As we grow, mature, and enter into a deeper understanding of God and his plan for humanity, we realize more fully than ever that God wants intact, loving families striving for heaven together. This is the beautiful ideal! But the fact is, we live in an imperfect world, and we may just find ourselves watching our dream of a happy family dissolving before our eyes.

During difficult times, we can either trust in God's mercy and work hard to preserve what we reasonably can, or we can buy into Satan's lies and settle for much less than what God wants for us. Good people, unused themselves to looking at things from the Christian perspective, are quick to offer poor advice which can sound like wisdom and tempt us to reject God's will for us. It is very appealing in our exhaustion, weakness, and desperation to look around and say, "Well, I guess this is just the way it is—everyone else seems to be doing okay following this less radical model of family life. My goals were unrealistic anyway."

We may have difficult-to-attain goals, but that doesn't mean we should abandon them when things start to go awry. And following God's commandments will always come at a price, no matter what state in life we are in. God is faithfully helping us in every situation to have the best family life we can, if we do not give up. During these times it is more important than ever to keep trusting with childlike simplicity in a God who desires our happiness and our salvation. He wants to give us a crown of beauty from the ashes of our hopes and dreams (see Isaiah 61:3).

So, no matter where we find ourselves in this moment in time, let's talk about the mission all Christian families have been given by God.

One day I was explaining to my children—most of whom were old enough to really "get" what I was saying—that our family has a mission from God. That, as a family, we can be the light of Christ and have an impact on others that we may never remotely perceive until we are in heaven. I offered them the example of a stone being cast into a pond and the ripple effect it produces. Our love of God and love of others as a family unit has great power to change the world. A few hours later, my smiling eleven-year-old showed me the first page of the library book he had just started reading.

The opening lines said, "Certain people have said that the world is like a calm pond, and that anytime a person does even the smallest thing, it is as if a stone has dropped into the pond, spreading circles of ripples further and further out, until the entire world has been changed by one tiny action."[2] God was confirming to my child, even at the tender age of eleven, that he has a role to play in our family's call to change the world.

When we mothers commit ourselves more deeply to God and walk with him daily, hopefully alongside our husbands, who are also called by God to holiness and *uniquely charged to lead the family*, we automatically have a core group to work with in building a faith community. This community of love and self-donation not only benefits each family member, but

---

[2] Lemony Snicket, *The Penultimate Peril*, Harper Collins 2005.

forms a team to do God's work. What an exciting adventure and mission!

I realize that it is rare that all team members are on board at all times, but that is the wonder of God's ways. He writes straight with crooked lines, so even if our family life is not the ideal, God will still use us. In fact, our imperfections and our families' particular struggles, if we let them, will make us uniquely equipped to share the mercy of God with others. We're on a mission from God, and each mission and each family has its place in God's divine plan!

Meditate

"All authority in heaven and on earth has been given to me. Go therefore and make disciples of all nations, baptizing them in the name of the Father and of the Son and of the Holy Spirit, teaching them to observe all that I have commanded you; and behold, I am with you always, to the close of the age."

Matthew 28:18-20

Consider

As the family goes, so goes the nation and so goes the whole world in which we live.

St. John Paul II

Pray

*Holy Trinity, One God, show me and my family
how to be a light to a world in darkness.*

* * * * *

Day Twenty-Eight

More Than Diplomas and Tight Abs

We have reached the end of our journey together. I hope you believe ever more deeply in your own worth as a daughter of God and are strengthened to chase the only dream worth pursuing—a life of holiness.

As we go on from here, it is so important to remember that living in a society that doesn't properly value the everyday heroism of motherhood can cripple us. We need to regularly meditate on and affirm God's plan for our vocation, otherwise disappointed utopian ideals of marriage and motherhood can trigger self-hate and anger. We may start to carry out the demands of family life reluctantly, with bitterness, feeling that somehow we have been cheated.

Most women want to follow their instincts and their consciences and become heroic mothers, but the prophets of doom in our world constantly whisper to us that giving ourselves away in self-donating love is loss of liberation. "It is no wonder you're so unhappy!" they hiss in our ear.

St. John Paul II had something to say about this voice that whispers lies to us. One day, my husband was reading one of John Paul II's encyclical letters while we sat in the parking lot of a convenience store waiting for one of the kids to emerge with (yet another) gallon of milk. When Pat showed me the following words of the Holy Father, I was moved to tears.

First, in this document, John Paul the Great reminds us of the abundant life we are offered in Christ and the value of *all* human life. He goes on to state that by making a total gift of ourselves to another we participate in "everyday heroism."

He underscores the difficulty of finding the meaning of motherhood in today's society:

> In living out their mission 'these heroic women do not always find support in the world around them. On the contrary, the cultural models frequently promoted and broadcast by the media do not encourage motherhood. In the name of progress and modernity the values of fidelity, chastity, sacrifice, to which a host of Christian wives and mothers have borne and continue to bear outstanding witness, are presented as obsolete. ... We thank you, heroic mothers, for your invincible love! ... We thank you for the sacrifice of your life. ... In the Paschal Mystery, Christ restores to you the gift you gave him. Indeed, he has the power to give you back the life you gave him as an offering.' (*Evangelium Vitae* 86)

This is the liberating truth: A life offered to God is the only life that can bring true freedom. When our days as wives and mothers become encounters with the living God, we begin to experience the kind of fulfillment that goes far deeper than a diploma on a wall, or the fact that we are forty-five and still have tight abs. What the world values is often ephemeral. But we know better.

Christian women, living virtuous and grace-filled lives, are particularly effective in whatever work we undertake. It is a marvelous thing that women have the capability, opportunity, and power to transform the world through the work that we do apart from our home and families. Such work may be essential to the well-being of countless individuals, including our own families, and, even if it is humble work, has value and dignity. *But for those of us whose are raising children at this particular point in our lives, the role of "mother" must take priority for the sake of our families and our world, and ultimately for our own well-being as we seek to do God's will.* We need to make choices, whenever possible, that will allow us the time and energy we need to meet our families' legitimate needs–choices that often contradict the "wisdom" of the day.

Most of us, in dedicating the majority of our time and energy to the needs of our families, can count on the fact that our lives will appear quite ordinary. Oprah will not be impressed and will not be calling us anytime soon. Motherhood lived out heroically does, though, have the capacity to make us holy; to perfect us in love. In so far as we can live out this call to love, we find true happiness. We also impact our family, and others with whom we come in contact, in a way that is sometimes subtle, especially at first; often striking, especially at the last, but always supernatural.

" It is no longer I who live, but Christ who lives in me" (Galatians 2:20).

Meditate

"I came that they might have life and have it abundantly."
John 10:10

Consider

And suddenly theories and speculation ended, and she knew. She knew that faithful, self-forgetting service, and the love that spends itself over and over, only to be renewed again and again, are the secret of happiness. For another world, perhaps leisure and beauty and luxury–but in this one, "Who loses his life shall gain it."
Kathleen Norris

Pray

All glory be to the Father and to the Son and to the Holy Spirit, as it was in the beginning is now and ever shall be, world without end. Amen.

About the Author

Besides being a wife, mother, and novice grandmother, Christine is a blogger, writing instructor, enthusiastic catechist and adequate gardener. She earned her BA in English Literature from the Franciscan University of Steubenville where she met her husband, Patrick. Over the years, they have lived in Nicaragua, New Mexico, Maryland, and then back to her roots in Upstate, New York.

Recently, the ups and downs of a bustling family life ended when their youngest child graduated high school. Christine and her husband aren't quite sure what the next phase of their lives will entail but have recently been traveling as much as possible to visit their loved ones scattered across the country. As followers of Jesus Christ, they do know this new phase in their life is guaranteed to be a grand adventure of love.

So, Catholic Mom, where do you go from here?

If you need more support and guidance for your family life (and who doesn't!), I urge you to tap into an organization like Messy Family Project. I believe so strongly in MFP's ministry to parents that I asked the co-founders to address you directly:

> We're Mike and Alicia Hernon from Messy Family Project. We're thrilled that your devotion to God and your family has prompted you to read a book like *Everyday Heroism*. We hope you were encouraged and inspired in your vocation as a woman and a mother and that God spoke to your heart through your quiet time with Him.
>
> Now it is time to think about ways you can continue to nurture and grow your Catholic family. We can help! Through parenting our 10 children and now as grandparents, we have learned (and continue to learn!) much about true love, sacrifice, and joy and we want to share that with you.
>
> **We do this through our blog, downloadable guides, videos, courses, and of course, our podcast which is now one of the top podcasts on Catholic parenting across the globe.** We want to inspire you with the gorgeous, God-given vista of Catholic marriage and family life. But we're not just here to point out the view; we're here to show you the path, point out the footholds, and equip you for the journey.
>
> Why are we so passionate about this? Because we believe that the Catholic family has what the whole world is looking for. And as we renew the family, we will transform the world.
>
> We would be honored to help you embrace the sacred calling of family life. **messyfamilyproject.org**

Made in the USA
Middletown, DE
25 April 2023

29441215R00097